speakout 2ND EDITION

Advanced
Workbook

with key

T0385942

Antonia Clare • JJ Wilson • Lindsay White

CONTENTS

CONTENTS

1)) ORIGINS

VOCABULARY

PHRASES WITH NAME

1 Complete the puzzle. Then reveal the key word to discover one of the world's most common names.

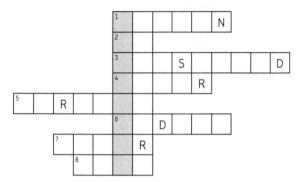

Clues

1 My married name is Lee, but my _____ name is Howarth.
2 With such famous parents it's hard to live _____ to my name.
3 All actors who go to Hollywood want to be _____ names.
4 My grandfather, George, was named _____ the King of England.
5 Theodorakopoulos? Is that a Greek _____?
6 My name's Max J. Hart. My _____ name is Joseph.
7 Following the accusation, I felt I needed to _____ my name.
8 After ten years in the job, it's time I _____ a name for myself.

GRAMMAR

THE CONTINUOUS ASPECT

2 A Read the article. Find and correct seven mistakes with the continuous aspect.

What's in a name?

People in the book business are always saying how difficult it is to think of a great title. There are so many books published these days that it's getting harder and harder. Recently, I'm walking through the aisles of a bookshop – I was hoping to find something for my grandmother's birthday – when I was noticing some very odd titles, some so clever that I had no idea what the book was about. If you've been working on your masterpiece for years, it seems such a shame that the book might get lost because of a poor title. Publishers are always telling would-be authors to keep the title short and descriptive, but I think there's more to it. The title is the first thing the reader is seeing and it has to be catchy. Jane Austen called one of her books *First Impressions*. I wonder if it would have been as famous if she hadn't been changing the title to *Pride and Prejudice*. William Golding wrote a novel called *Strangers from Within*. That's OK, but I'm preferring what it later became – *Lord of the Flies*. Famously, Paul McCartney had been working on a melody when he decided to give it the working title *Scrambled Eggs*. Fortunately, The Beatles changed it. *Yesterday* is now a classic. Anyway, I think of writing a book called *How to Name your Book*. It's something I've planned for at least ten minutes and I'm expecting it to make me millions.

B Read the blog again. Underline seven examples of the continuous aspect used correctly. Why is the continuous used in these examples? Match them with uses a)–e).

a) to describe a background action that was in progress when another (shorter) action happened
b) to talk about something that is incomplete, temporary or still in progress (often emphasising the length of time)
c) to talk about situations that are in the process of changing
d) to emphasise repeated actions (that may be annoying)
e) for plans that may not be definite

3 Underline the correct alternative.

1 When she saw Jan, she knew immediately that he had *cried/been crying*.
2 Dad, I *wondered/was wondering* if I could borrow your car this weekend.
3 We'd already *eaten/been eating* all our food and we still had two more days of travel.
4 Because of the poor economy, it *is getting/gets* more difficult to find work.
5 Are you free tomorrow? I *hope/was hoping* you might help me with my tax forms.
6 I've *owned/been owning* six houses in my lifetime, but this is by far the best.
7 This room is filthy! What have you *been doing/done* all morning?
8 At the first signs of trouble, animals *always move/are always moving* to higher ground.
9 The boss *always tells/is always telling* us to work hard, but she does nothing.
10 You should ask Don. He may *know/be knowing* some good restaurants.
11 Helga and I *are thinking/think* of moving to Spain. What do you reckon?
12 Look at this car. We've *tried/been trying* to fix it for weeks!

LISTENING

4 A Look at the pictures. How might these be connected to stories of people's names?

B ▶ **1.1** Listen to six people talking about their names and check your answers.

C Answer the questions, then listen again to check.

1 Why did Speaker 1 'revert to Felipe'?
What name is on his official documents?

_____

2 What did Speaker 2 think of her real name?
What did she do later?

_____

3 What did Speaker 3's parents decide to do?
What problem did they discover later?

_____

4 How do you spell Speaker 4's name?
What part of the body does it sound like?

_____

5 What is good and bad about Speaker 5's name?
What does he say about his parents?

_____

6 Why does Speaker 6 describe her name as 'a nightmare'? Where is her surname from?

_____

D Complete the summary with the expressions in the box.

> are absolutely baffled   of a compromise
> the mists of time   now plain old
> an act of defiance   a mixed blessing

Speaker 1, Felipe, changed his name as
¹_____, a way to rebel against authority.
Speaker 2 had a long 'hippy' name, but is
²_____ Summer Davies, which is much simpler.
Speaker 3, David Donald, got his name as a result
³_____ between his parents, who wanted to call him different names.
Speaker 4 says people ⁴_____ by her name because the pronunciation differs from the way it is spelt, which makes it confusing.
Speaker 5 says his name is ⁵_____ – there are good and bad things about being called James Bond.
Speaker 6 says the origins of her surname have been lost in ⁶_____ – she doesn't know when or how the story of her surname was forgotten.

WRITING

A PERSONAL PROFILE; LEARN TO PLAN YOUR WRITING

5 A Read the advertisement and think about the personal and professional qualities required for the job.

> ### GST Adventure Camp
> ### Summer job: Ontario, Canada
>
> Instructors needed for children's summer camp, June 18–July 22
>
> The mission of GST Adventure Camp is to teach new skills, develop children's confidence and teach the value of cooperation. The children are aged 6–16.
>
> Applicants must be proficient in all kinds of outdoor activities, e.g. camping, fishing, swimming, kayaking, rock climbing.
>
> Please send a CV and personal profile stating your interests, skills and experience with children of all ages. Also tell us about your character. Applicants must be 18+.
>
> **All camps are held in and around Beaverton, Ontario, by Lake Simcoe.**

B Read this outline of a personal profile for the job. What information is irrelevant? What information is missing? Read the advertisement again to help you.

> **Introduction:** my background, age
>
> **Interests:** outdoor living, e.g. fishing, cooking; collecting stamps from different countries
>
> **Skills:** good climber, swimmer and sailor; proficient in Word, Excel, PowerPoint
>
> **Experience:** worked for Dream Campers, July 2014, looking after fifteen eight-year-olds.

C Write a personal profile for the job (200 words).

VOCABULARY
PERSONALITY

1 Complete the sentences with the words in the box. You don't need to use all the words.

> thoughtful perceptive obsessive inspirational obstinate
> over-ambitious conscientious neurotic solitary mature
> prejudiced apathetic insensitive inquisitive open-minded

1 Clara has always been particularly _____. She's always asking questions.
2 I can't believe that he didn't realise how upset you are. How _____ of him.
3 I know that we can rely on them to get the job finished on time. They are very _____.
4 I'm quite a _____ person so I love having a weekend with no social engagements.
5 I was prone to being rather _____ as a child. I would regularly refuse to do what I was told.
6 My mother is completely _____. She worries about the most ridiculous things.
7 I'm not sure that Kevin is really _____ enough to make the right decision. He seems very young for his age.
8 You mustn't be _____ and take on impossible tasks. Make sure that your goals are achievable.
9 My grandmother is extremely _____ about what women should and shouldn't do. She thinks it's terrible that I'm an engineer.
10 She's obviously very _____. She knew exactly what we were talking about and made a few comments that nobody else would have thought of.
11 He has wonderfully original ideas. He's _____ to work with.
12 I'm not sure what the problem is, but Tomas seems very _____ in his work recently. He's just not getting round to doing it.

GRAMMAR
DESCRIBING HABITS

2 Circle the correct option to complete the sentences.

1 I have a _____ to get people's names mixed up.
   a) tendency **b)** inclined **c)** prone
2 Aaliya _____ hours in the bathroom getting ready. It drives me crazy.
   a) tend to spend **b)** will spend **c)** is spending
3 Grandad is _____ to getting lost and being brought home by the police.
   a) prone **b)** inclined **c)** tending
4 I mostly _____ to read when I'm on holiday.
   a) have tendency **b)** tend **c)** am tending
5 They would keep _____ me to move offices. So, in the end, I left.
   a) to ask **b)** ask **c)** asking
6 People _____ sending me emails asking for advice.
   a) always **b)** always are **c)** were always

3 Find and correct the mistake in nine of the sentences.

1 My mobile phone company keeps call me every day. It's driving me crazy.
2 Beatrix is always ask us to come and visit.
3 I'll always have a coffee as soon as I wake up.
4 My aunt would coming and collect us from school and take us to her house for the weekend.
5 As rule, I like to try a recipe out on my family first, before I invite people round to eat it.
6 I have an incline to be rather disorganised.
7 I tend agree with everything they say. It makes things easier.
8 I'll generally read through everything at least twice before signing.
9 Nine times of ten, he'll be home by 6.30, but occasionally he'll get stuck in traffic.
10 She's forever leaving the car unlocked – it'll get stolen one day.
11 My brother used to apathetic about his studies but he's much more conscientious now.
12 As a teenager, I was always argue with my parents.

READING

4 A Read the article opposite. Choose the best summary.

A People who don't smile enough at work are trying to conceal their own incompetence.
B You can improve your success at work by smiling more to ingratiate yourself with others.
C Too much smiling can make you appear incompetent.

B Read the article again. Are the statements true (T) or false (F)?

1 The writer smiled to get out of difficult situations in previous jobs.
2 Smiling at customers to cover up your incompetence can be a good habit to acquire.
3 The journalist interviewed successful businesswomen regarding the key to their success.
4 She was not particularly surprised by what they told her.
5 There is a stereotype which assumes that if you are being nice to someone, you are probably not very competent at your job.
6 Using direct language, rather than soft language, in your emails may help to affirm your authority and give an air of competence.

Take that smile OFF your face

Are you too nice for your own good? When I had my first job as a waitress in a restaurant, I soon learnt that the best way to get myself out of trouble was to smile sweetly at every possible opportunity. 'I'm so sorry,' I beamed, when I dropped the plate on the floor and it smashed into **smithereens**. 'There must have been a misunderstanding. I'll sort it out straightaway,' I smiled, having served chicken kiev to a strict vegetarian. It came naturally. Smiling was a necessary part of the job, dealing with customers – but when I look back at the experience now, I can see that what I was actually doing was desperately covering up for my own inadequacies, my incompetence. I had no idea what I was really supposed to be doing, so I'd smile nicely and hope I would get through the day alive. And it quickly became a habit that stuck.

In fact, it's a habit that has stayed with me for nearly twenty years. Recently, I interviewed a group of top businesswomen about what they felt was the key factor in their success. Was it their acute **business acumen**, their nerves of steel in the boardroom, their ability to spot an opportunity when it arose? I was completely **caught off guard** and quite **taken aback** when one woman, Miriam, a highly successful manager of a top football club, explained to me how she had survived and prospered in a particularly male-dominated environment. 'You have to learn to stop smiling,' she said. 'You don't need to make people like you all the time. You just have to do your job and do it well. And the job isn't just about being nice.'

It's so simple but I had never really stopped to notice. You see, by smiling, what you're really doing is trying to ingratiate yourself with the other person. It's a submissive gesture. And in business, people who appear warm and friendly may be perceived as being less competent compared to others who appear cold, hard and **aloof**. In fact, there have been numerous studies done demonstrating the stereotype that people tend to see warmth and competence as inversely related. If there is an apparent **surplus** of one trait, then it is assumed that there will be a **deficit** of the other.

The effect is not just limited to smiling, either. Think about all the emoticons and soft language we use to make our emails more 'friendly'. After my meeting with Miriam, I frantically searched back through my recent correspondence and found, to my dismay, that my emails were littered with apologies and covert requests. 'I'm terribly sorry to have to ask you …', 'Do you think you could possibly …?', 'I wondered if it might be all right to just …?'. So, I've taken an executive decision. From now on I will be more assertive and direct with the people I work with. I've removed all **niceties** from my emails – and I've wiped that permanent smile from my face. ~~Thanks for reading!~~☺

C Complete the sentences with the words and phrases in bold from the article. Use the definitions in brackets to help you.

1 I was completely _____. I didn't expect it at all. (surprised)

2 The new manager walked into the room. And without any _____ at all, he started the meeting. (polite social behaviour)

3 He took a hammer and smashed the plate into _____. (many very small pieces)

4 I've always been afraid to talk to her. She seems very _____. (distant and remote)

5 If, at the end of the month, there are any _____ funds, we can use them to hold a celebration dinner. (extra)

6 I was rather _____ by the suggestion. (shocked)

7 With his remarkable _____, I'm sure he will be fantastically successful. (insight into business)

8 It was an attempt to reduce the budget _____. (the amount by which a sum of money falls short of a reference amount)

VOCABULARY PLUS

IDIOMS FOR PEOPLE

5 Complete the conversations with the words in the box.

body	box	horse	kid	neck	sheep	soul	ways

1 A: Who told you about Ali and Pietro getting married? It was supposed to be a secret.
   B: Sorry, Anne told me. She can be a bit of a busy_____.

2 A: I'm so glad Pilar is coming tonight. She'll get everyone going.
   B: Yes, she tends to be the life and _____ of the party.

3 A: All my family are academics but I left school when I was fifteen.
   B: Yeah, you've always been the black _____ of the family.

4 A: She hasn't stopped talking for the last two and a half hours!
   B: I know. She's a terrible chatter_____.

5 A: I'm not sure how the team will respond to these new ideas.
   B: Do you think they're a bit set in their _____?

6 A: You didn't tell me that Andreas was in a rock band!
   B: I didn't know. He's quite a dark _____.

7 A: I can't work out how this computer program works.
   B: Why don't you ask Dan? He's a whizz_____ when it comes to computers.

8 A: He's one of our customers but he seems to enjoy complaining.
   B: Are you saying he's a pain in the _____?

VOCABULARY

IMAGES

1 Underline the correct alternative.

1 The image of the exhausted soldiers was frighteningly *iconic/striking*.

2 He found the portraits of the boys on the beach *provocative/evocative* of his childhood holidays.

3 We went to an exhibition of *revealing/iconic* portraits by unknown photographers.

4 The close-up *revealing/captures the beauty* of the model, doesn't it?

5 I find her work shocking. It's too *provocative/iconic*.

6 Dorothea Lange took some of the most *captures the beauty/iconic* pictures of 1930s USA.

FUNCTION

SPECULATING

2 Match the beginnings of conversations 1–6 with the responses a)–f).

1 Do you think there's any chance that we'll win the cup?

2 What's that on the horizon? Can you see?

3 Have you got the time on you?

4 What do you think about that hotel over there?

5 It's Mahbek. He wants to know when we'll get there.

6 Have you seen the queue?

a) Yes, it gives me the impression that we might have to wait for some time.

b) I'd say that it's definitely expensive. Look at those chandeliers!

c) No, I haven't. But I'd hazard a guess that it's about lunchtime.

d) If I had to make a guess, I'd say we'll be with him in an hour.

e) I reckon there's a fair chance of it, yeah. We've played well all season.

f) I wonder if it could be a fishing boat.

3 Look at the pictures. Make two sentences about each one using the prompts.

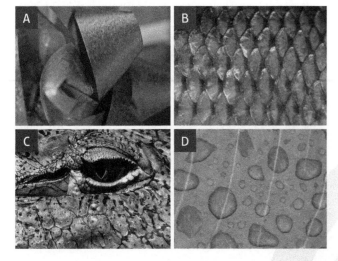

1 guess / could / be
_____

2 hazard / guess / that
_____

3 wonder / if
_____

4 reckon / it
_____

5 seems / to / me
_____

6 gives / impression / that
_____

7 pretty sure / it
_____

8 had / make / guess / say
_____

LEARN TO

USE VAGUE LANGUAGE

4 A ▶ 1.2 Listen to the conversation. Are the statements true (T) or false (F)?

1 Anna is on her way to visit Francesca.

2 They are planning to go out to eat somewhere.

3 Anna can't stand spicy food.

B Listen again. What exactly do they say? Complete the extracts.

1 I'll see you here at about _____ then.

2 I need to pick up a _____ of things …

3 I've got plenty of _____ to be getting on with here.

4 I've just got to finish some work and sort the kitchen out and stuff _____.

5 Do you want me to bring anything, you _____, …

6 … any kind of food or _____ like that?

7 Oh, there's one _____ I was going to ask.

8 Are you OK with spicy food? You know, chilli and _____?

C Find examples of vague language in the sentences above and write them under the headings below.

vague nouns: (e.g. *thing, stuff, bit, something*)
_____

quantifiers: (e.g. *one or two, a few, a couple of, a lot*)
_____

vague numbers: (e.g. *around, about fifty, more or less*)
_____

generalisers: (e.g. *sort of, kind of, you know*)
_____

list completers: (e.g. *and stuff, and so on, or something*)
_____

2)) OPINION

VOCABULARY

LEARNING AND EXPERIENCE

1 Write one word in each gap to complete the texts.

The **best** advice **I've** ever **received**

AHMED SAEED WAHABI
(POLITICIAN)

'When I was growing up, we would get five newspapers every day from all sides of the political spectrum. I asked my father why we needed five newspapers and he said 'so we can see everyone's point of view'. This had a profound [1] _____ on me. Now, whenever I face a tricky situation, I look at it from the other side's point of view. This helps me understand the issue fully and take [2] _____ of the opportunity in front of me.'

RICHARD HALLIDAY
(INVESTOR)

'When I was [3] _____ the ropes, I met a legendary billionaire investor. I asked him the secret of his success and he said, 'I'm not a smart guy. I just read everything: trade magazines, financial news, annual reports, even the footnotes in annual reports. That's why I know more than 98 percent of people on Wall Street.' He was right. Now I read everything. Once you have all the information, you can [4] _____ your instincts.'

CLARE NICHOLAS
(CEO)

'When I first became a high-level manager, I was on a steep [5] _____ curve. A colleague said to me, 'I see you in meetings. You're very intelligent, but you don't know enough about the industry. Don't be too proud to ask if you don't understand something.' I followed his advice. When you're finding your [6] _____ it's better to ask than to bluff.'

GRAMMAR

HYPOTHETICAL CONDITIONAL: PAST

2 Circle the correct options to complete the text.

Regrets – just a few

President Theodore Roosevelt once said, 'The only time you really live fully is from thirty to sixty. The young are slaves to dreams; the old [are] servants of regrets.' Indeed, it's often claimed that young people wish they [1] _____ the things they did and old people regret not doing the things they didn't do.

A very informal poll among friends and acquaintances for this column reveals that people generally regret [2] _____ (more) children, choosing the wrong career and missing out on the man or woman of their dreams. Then there are the odd, individual cases.

A close friend said, 'I wish [3] _____ become a vegetarian earlier. [4] _____ I done so, over the years I'd have saved about 400 chickens, 50 pigs and 30 cows.'

Another pal said, 'If I [5] _____ such an idiot when I was eighteen, I'd never have had this tattoo done. Imagine spending your whole life with a picture of your ex-girlfriend on your arm. If only it [6] _____ Mother Teresa or someone who deserves to be there!'

I spoke to an ex-professional footballer whose career was cut short by injury. 'If I'd been smarter, I [7] _____ put all my eggs in one basket. I [8] _____ at least finished school. Aged twenty-seven, I had no qualifications apart from kicking a ball.'

Of my elderly contacts, about half wished [9] _____ followed their passion instead of taking the safe option. One grandfather-of-fifteen said, 'I might [10] _____ a good actor, but at the time I had a big family to support and acting isn't a secure profession. So I became a bank clerk and spent the rest of my life cashing other people's cheques.'

As an antidote to all this doom and gloom, another friend cheerfully said, 'Regrets? If only we [11] _____ how good life is.' Then he told me that people should make lists of all the friends they've had, the places they've seen, the things they've enjoyed. 'I wish everyone [12] _____ the good things in life!' he said and drained his cup of tea in one gulp.

1 a) hadn't been doing **b)** hadn't done **c)** are doing
  d) have done
2 a) to have **b)** of not having **c)** not having
  d) not to have
3 a) I was **b)** I'm **c)** I've **d)** I'd
4 a) If **b)** Had **c)** Have **d)** Should
5 a) hadn't been **b)** had been **c)** didn't be
  d) not been
6 a) were **b)** was being **c)** 's been **d)** wasn't
7 a) didn't **b)** wouldn' **c)** wouldn't have
  d) would have
8 a) have **b)** must have **c)** would **d)** 'd have
9 a) they'd **b)** they **c)** they did **d)** they'd been
10 a) have been becoming **b)** have become
  c) had become **d)** become
11 a) realise **b)** can realise **c)** realised
  d) are realising
12 a) has appreciated **b)** is appreciating
  c) appreciates **d)** would appreciate

3 Match 1–8 with a)–h) to make sentences.

1 We wouldn't have got here so early had we
2 They would have lost the match but
3 Supposing you'd been offered a part in that film,
4 Tom wouldn't be sitting here right now if
5 If only the Johnsons had never
6 Imagine you'd really lost your ticket, how would
7 I think all of us regret
8 I really wish I

a) would you have accepted?
b) you have got home?
c) not being nicer to Mandy.
d) hadn't said those things to Mum.
e) I hadn't pulled him through that window.
f) for Thomson's goal at the end.
g) known you weren't going to be here until 6.00.
h) bought that house, they wouldn't be in debt now.

4 A ▶ 2.1 Listen and complete the sentences with the words you hear. Some words are contractions.

1 I _____ _____ _____ more when I was younger.
2 If _____ _____ _____ met that crazy man!
3 If I'd had more talent, _____ _____ _____ famous.
4 I wouldn't be here _____ _____ _____ to my parents.
5 If it wasn't for you, _____ _____ _____ about that flat.
6 _____ _____ _____ the scholarship, would you have gone?

B Practise saying the sentences to yourself at full speed.

C Write six sentences. Include the words you wrote in Exercise 4A. Say your sentences aloud, making sure you say the contracted forms.

I wish I'd studied English at school because I need it for my job.

VOCABULARY PLUS

METAPHORS

5 Sentences 1–8 each have a word missing. Complete the sentences with the words in the box.

at	downhill	for	go	ideas	of	~~regurgitate~~	to

                                              regurgitate
1 I hate exams in which you just have to ∧ the teacher's ideas.
2 Although she was at the peak her career, she decided to take a year off.
3 My tennis has gone as I've got older.
4 I was a crossroads in my career so I had to make a move.

5 I find a lot of his theories rather hard swallow.
6 When I joined the company, my boss said, 'You'll far.'
7 This report says human cloning is only a few years away. Hmm, that's food thought.
8 He emails me with these ridiculous half-baked on how to improve the business.

LISTENING

6 A Look at the photo. What can you guess about this woman's life?

1 Is she rich or poor?
2 Does she have a family?
3 Where is she from?
4 Do people like her?
5 What did she teach herself to do?

B ▶ 2.2 Listen and answer the questions above.

C Write questions for answers 1–6. Then listen again to check.

1 _____
   When she was six years old.
2 _____
   He was a tailor.
3 _____
   Five.
4 _____
   One year.
5 _____
   She thought it was a hoax.
6 _____
   Eight hundred.

D Match the underlined words and expressions from the recording with the definitions a)–f). Read the audio script on page 74 to help you.

1 'she'd sailed to Brazil at the age of six with nothing but the <u>rags</u> on her back'
2 'cars, the new <u>playthings</u> of the wealthy'
3 [She was] 'a <u>prolific</u> producer of babies'
4 'She had <u>an iron will</u>'
5 'she turned into the neighbourhood <u>fairy godmother</u>'
6 'don't wash your dirty <u>linen</u> in public'

a) great determination
b) laundry
c) imaginary person who makes your dreams come true
d) material that is in very bad condition (ripped or out of shape)
e) toys
f) extremely productive

READING

1 A Read the blog. Have you read or heard of any of the books which are mentioned?

B Which type of book is not mentioned?
a) a novel about a young girl
b) a non-fictional account of an expedition
c) a detailed biography of a scientist
d) an autobiographical history
e) a philosophical memoir

2 Which of the books:

1 gave the reader new insights into a different culture?
_____

2 inspired the reader to go on a journey?
_____

3 challenges the orthodox views of western science?
_____

4 was read by a young reader?
_____

5 describes how the culture of a country is changing as seen through the eyes of three women?
_____

6 discusses issues of social justice and poverty?
_____

7 describes the struggle of two men trying to achieve something which had not been previously achieved?
_____

8 encourages you to rethink scientific values?
_____

3 Find words and phrases in the article which mean:

1 to be a typical example of something (introduction)
_____

2 so excited or interested that you are reluctant to stop (*Wild Swans*) _____

3 full of poverty (*To Kill a Mocking Bird*) _____

4 making you feel sad or full of pity (*To Kill a Mocking Bird*) _____

5 statement or idea on which you base other ideas (*Zen and the Art of Motorcycle Maintenance*)
_____

6 land that is always wet or covered with water (*To the Ends of the Earth*) _____

Books that BLEW your mind

Every once in a while there will be a book that makes you want to shout out from the rooftops 'Read this book!' They are the books that just blow your mind. Perhaps they epitomise your spirit of adventure or challenge some long-held perception you have. Maybe they quite simply change your way of thinking forever. Sounds familiar? Then share your ideas with the rest of us!

Wild Swans: Three Daughters of China
Jung Chang

I remember reading this whilst on holiday with a boyfriend. I was absolutely gripped by the book, unable to put it down at the breakfast table, during our sightseeing trips and well into the night. It's an autobiographical account of three female generations of Chang's family and I was fascinated by the picture it painted of Chinese culture, the things that happened during the Cultural Revolution and how China is changing now. It was a truly eye-opening read.

Lori, San Francisco

To Kill a Mocking Bird
Harper Lee

We had to read this at school as one of our set texts. Until that time, I'd never been particularly interested in reading, but I remember being so moved by the story of Atticus and his fight for justice. The story, set in poverty-ridden Alabama during the depression, is told through the eyes of Atticus' young daughter (Scout) and I wonder if it was this that made the story so poignant for me, reading it as a young schoolgirl myself. Interestingly, although this book won her huge acclaim, it was 55 years before Harper Lee wrote another novel.

Maxine, Oxford

Zen and the Art of Motorcycle Maintenance
Robert M. Pirsig

This book has sold more than 5 million copies worldwide, making it one of the biggest-selling philosophy books ever. In the book, Pirsig explores many themes, and one of them is the whole premise on which science, and therefore western medicine, is based. It's a book about questioning and the search for true meaning, and for me it was quite simply a revelation. It opened my eyes to a new way of thinking. There are some books you need to read as you're growing up and this, for me, was one of them.

Luke, Sydney

To the Ends of the Earth
Ranulph Fiennes

This book was quite literally life-changing for me. The book describes the Transglobe Expedition undertaken in 1979 by adventurers Ranulph Fiennes and Charles R. Burton. This 100,000-mile journey from pole to pole, took them across the Sahara, through the swamps and jungles of Mali and the Ivory Coast and over unexplored areas of Antarctica. The book describes how the two men risked death in order to achieve something spectacular and it was this that first inspired me to complete a solo transatlantic sailing trip myself.

Alex, Dublin

VOCABULARY

COLLOCATIONS: OPINIONS

4 Complete the sentences with the words in the box.

> stereotype   eye-opening   second thoughts
> convincing   an open mind   perspective
> narrow-minded   preconceptions

1 The _____ I had about life in South Africa were the same as many people have.
2 She doesn't fit the _____ of what a good mother is.
3 Originally, he accepted the promotion, but then he had _____.
4 It's vital that we keep _____ about what might have happened.
5 I found the professors at the university to be incredibly _____. They weren't prepared to accept new ways of thinking.
6 My travels in South America were an _____ experience. I learnt so much about the culture of the people and how it is different from my own.
7 I think we need to look at the situation from a new _____.
8 The evidence of his guilt was not very _____.

GRAMMAR

VERB PATTERNS

5 Complete the sentences with the correct form of the verbs in brackets.

1 As a business leader, _____ (make) decisions is one of the most important things you do.
2 The fact is that circumstances change all the time. You may need to contemplate _____ (change) your decision.
3 If the facts and environment change, you need _____ (be) willing and able to make changes quickly while you still have the chance _____ (do) so.
4 The scientists appear _____ (steal) their research from another source.
5 The officer in question was reported _____ (change) his account of the events on many occasions.
6 I would hate _____ (have to) miss an opportunity like that. Can't you change the date?
7 Paula was forever _____ (give) bad advice by her superiors.
8 Not _____ (have) the courage of your convictions can be seen as a weakness.
9 The directors seem _____ (reach) the same conclusion as we did.

WRITING

A DISCURSIVE ESSAY; LEARN TO USE LINKING DEVICES

6 A Choose the correct alternatives to complete the first draft of a discursive essay.

> # Globalisation will eventually lead to a complete loss of cultural identity
>
> People around the world are becoming increasingly similar. ¹*In fact,/However,/For this reason*, they often eat the same food, watch the same TV programmes and wear the same clothes.
>
> ²*Another problem is/As a result,/Conversely*, it could be said that cultural identities are in danger of being lost. ³*However,/For this reason,/In addition to this*, cultural identity is about much more than the clothes you wear. The foundation of cultural identity lies in the values we share with others.
>
> ⁴*On the contrary,/Nevertheless,/What is more*, as global brands become ever more prominent, it's easy to imagine how this trend will continue until, eventually, we lose all traces of our own cultural identity.
>
> ⁵*On the other hand,/Additionally,/Accordingly*, global integration together with improved travel and communication systems mean that it is becoming increasingly easy for people to learn and understand more about different cultures and to broaden their own cultural horizons. ⁶*Nevertheless,/Consequently,/Obviously*, cultural identity continues to play a vital role in people's lives, reminding them of their associated history and ancestors.
>
> ⁷*Obviously,/However,/Furthermore*, it has also become apparent that in a significant number of countries, people feel that their traditional way of life is getting lost as a result of foreign influence …

B Look at the essay again. Are the sentences 1–7 for (✓) or against (✗) the argument?

C Write the final draft of the essay (200–250 words) using the first draft as a starting point. Add further examples to the discursive essay using some of the linking devices you discarded in Exercise 6A.

VOCABULARY

IDIOMS OF OPINION

1 A Correct the idioms.

a) play devil's attorney _____

b) sit on the wall _____

c) speak your thoughts _____

d) beat about the garden _____

e) have a vested motivation _____

f) have an axe to sharpen _____

B Match the idioms in Exercise 1A with their definitions.

1 have a private motive for doing something

2 talk a lot without directly addressing the most important point

3 say what you really believe

4 be unable to commit yourself to one opinion or one side

5 a special interest in an existing system, arrangement or institution for particular personal reasons

6 say something unlikely or unpopular so people will think about the issue more carefully

C Complete the sentences with the correct idioms.

1 You can't _____ for ever. At some stage you need to decide whose side you're on.

2 He has a _____ in the industry so I don't think he should serve on the regulating board.

3 I feel I must _____. This proposal is absolutely terrible and it makes no sense!

4 I'd like to _____. What if we lose all our clients to our competitor? What happens then?

5 Let's not _____. This film was a disaster.

6 Every time she speaks to me, she mentions last year's salary cuts. She really has an _____.

FUNCTION

INTRODUCING OPINIONS

2 Cross out the extra word in each statement.

1 If you want for my honest opinion, I think smoking should be made illegal.

2 There are no miracle diets. Look at it on this way: those diet ads are selling you an impossible dream.

3 From what that I can gather, global warming is a very real problem. If we don't address it now, it'll be too late.

4 By according to the government, immigration is out of control. The reality is, immigrants bring many skills.

5 Quite clearly frankly, I think military service is a great idea. Young people today need the kind of discipline that the army brings.

6 If you will ask me, hunting should be banned. In the eyes of any humane person, it's an inhumane 'sport'.

3 Write sentences with the same meaning as the sentences below. Use the words in brackets.

1 In truth, corruption is a huge problem. (reality / is)

_____

2 The results show that the experiment was a success. (according / to)

_____

3 In my view, Kurt is the best candidate. (far / concerned)

_____

4 I hear that the company will merge next year. (from / gather)

_____

5 As I understand it, he disagreed with everything his boss said. (to / knowledge)

_____

6 In my opinion, his early songs are much better than the later stuff. (ask / me)

_____

7 Without beating about the bush, I think she's a genius. (frankly)

_____

LEARN TO

EXPRESS DOUBT

4 A Put the underlined words in the correct order to complete the conversation.

A: Did you hear about the archaeological findings in Ethiopia? An anthropologist claims to have found 'the missing link'.

B: Really? ¹unlikely / that / find / I / highly. Anthropologists are always saying they've made these wonderful discoveries and mostly it's nonsense.

A: Anyway, this anthropologist found some bones which were unlike anything ever found before and …

B: ²don't / that / know / I / about. A bone is a bone is a bone.

A: Yes, but these were a different structure. And …

B: ³really / about / sure / I'm / that / not. A different structure? What was it: a human with wings or something?

A: No! ⁴idea / you / where / that / did / get? It was a skeleton that didn't look like either a human or a chimpanzee but it was over four million years old.

B: ⁵debatable / very / that's. Four million years? How do they know?

A: I give up. What's on TV?

B ▶ 2.3 Listen and check.

C ▶ 2.4 Listen and repeat sentences 1–5 from Exercise 4A. Concentrate on the intonation for expressing doubt (e.g. long vowel sounds on *really* and *highly*).

GRAMMAR THE CONTINUOUS ASPECT

1 Underline the correct alternatives. Sometimes both options are possible.

'My name's Amanda. It ¹*comes/'s coming* from the Latin, meaning "worthy of love". It's interesting because I ²*study/'m studying* Latin at the moment, so that gives it some extra resonance for me.'

'My surname is Russell, though originally, it was Rosen, which is a German name. My grandfather ³*changed/was changing* his name when he ⁴*moved/was moving* to the UK just before the Second World War.'

'My name is Max Clare, which I ⁵*found/ was finding* very difficult as a young boy. At school, the teachers would call us by our surnames and, as a result, the other kids ⁶*always teased/always were teasing* me and ⁷*called/calling* me "Clare".'

'I have a rather unusual surname and it's made worse by the fact that I'm a doctor. I'm Dr Tooth, which always ⁸*makes/is making* people laugh. I suppose it could have been worse though – at one point I ⁹*planned/was planning* to become a dentist. Luckily, I changed my mind.'

'I've ¹⁰*thought/been thinking* about changing my name for a while now. I've never ¹¹*liked/been liking* my name and it doesn't hold happy memories for me. So, now I'm an adult, I thought I could choose a name which I prefer.'

'We ¹²*hoped/were hoping* you could help us to decide on a name for the company. At the moment we ¹³*consider/'re considering* various options.'

VOCABULARY REVIEW 1

2 Complete the pairs of sentences with the correct word or phrase.

1 live up to/make
   a) It must have been hard for someone like Ziggy Marley to _____ his name.
   b) She's working hard trying to _____ a name for herself in show business.

2 put your name forward/clear your name
   a) The lawyers are trying to _____ so that you can continue to work in this area.
   b) It was good of you to _____ for the role of chairperson.

3 household name/maiden name
   a) As a singer, he became a _____ after his hugely successful debut album.
   b) My mother's _____ was Glinka.

4 perceptive/inspirational
   a) We left the _____ talk feeling positive and motivated.
   b) I thought her report on the links between poverty and crime was most _____.

5 conscientious/apathetic
   a) Politically, I'm rather _____ because I don't feel that my opinion has any influence.
   b) He is an extraordinarily _____ worker and usually the last person to leave the building.

6 prejudiced/rebellious
   a) He can be rather _____ against minorities.
   b) At school he was renowned for having a _____ character.

7 solitary/inquisitive
   a) Harry would rather spend time alone. He's a _____ personality.
   b) They ask questions about everything. They are so _____.

8 obstinate/neurotic
   a) She can be very _____ about things so it's difficult to persuade her to change her mind once she's decided.
   b) They worry far too much. They're completely _____ about everything.

9 provocative/revealing
   a) The tour photographer got some _____ images of the band relaxing after the concerts.
   b) The artist has received lots of complaints about her _____ exhibition but I think she is enjoying the negative publicity.

10 striking/iconic
   a) She managed to get several _____ photographs of the sunrise.
   b) The gallery shop only sold postcards of the most _____ pictures in their collection.

GRAMMAR DESCRIBING HABITS

3 Correct the sentences by adding, removing or changing one word.

1 Nine times of ten he'll be right, but that is no guarantee.

2 I was forever have to apologise for his behaviour.

3 Kids are prone for to eat too much junk food.

4 Greg has tendency to be critical, which makes him unpopular with his co-workers.

5 As a ruler, most students finish their coursework by the end of May.

6 I'll generally to have just a piece of toast for breakfast.

7 She was not inclined get up early on a Sunday morning.

8 When we were younger we would spend for hours just playing in the garden.

VOCABULARY PLUS IDIOMS FOR PEOPLE

4 Complete the sentences with the words in the box.

black busybodies chatterbox hand
whizzkids life neck ways

1 I would ask Graham. He's an old _____ when it comes to things like this.

2 Giada has always been the _____ sheep of the family. She's such a rebel.

3 To be the _____ and soul of the party you need to come out of your shell and let go.

4 Marcos was sixty-five and rather set in his _____ about how to do things.

5 The city is full of financial _____.

6 My neighbours drive me crazy. They are real _____, always poking their noses in your business.

7 You'll have to tell me if I'm talking too much. I tend to be a bit of a _____.

8 The customs officer refused to let us through. He was a real pain in the _____.

FUNCTION SPECULATING

5 Underline the correct alternative.

1 I'll *hazardous/I'd hazard a* guess that there'll be some kind of confrontation.

2 It *make/makes* me think that maybe they were right all along.

3 I *suppose/supposing* they've probably finished by now.

4 I'd *reckoning/I reckon* they're going to win.

5 I'm *sure pretty/pretty sure* they would have asked us if we had to leave.

6 She *gives/makes* the impression of always being very calm.

VOCABULARY REVIEW 2

6 Add vowels to complete the phrases.

1 I'm just a beginner. I'm l__rn__ng th__ r_p__s.

2 When you're not sure about a decision, you just need to tr__st y__r __nst__ncts.

3 I'm really enjoying my new job, but it's been a st__p l__rn__ng c__rv__.

4 I was planning to have a big party to celebrate but now I'm having s__c__nd th__ghts.

5 We don't know what is going to happen so we need to keep an op__n m__nd about things.

6 Let's try to look at the situation from a wh__l__ n__w p__rsp__ct__v__.

7 I can't stand it when people are so n__rr__w-m__nd__d.

8 Don't worry about me. I'm just playing d__v__l's __dv__c__t__.

9 You can rely on Fernandez to sp__ __k h__s m__nd.

10 It's no use b__ __t__ng __b__ __t th__ b__sh. Just get to the point.

GRAMMAR HYPOTHETICAL CONDITIONAL: PAST

7 Complete the sentences using the prompts. There may be more than one possible answer.

1 never / meet
If I hadn't gone to the USA, I
_____ my husband.

2 not / have to / call
If only we'd known about the spare key, we
_____ the police.

3 not / just / go
Had we realised that the interview had started, we
_____ into the room without knocking.

4 you / do
Supposing you'd been in my shoes, what
_____ when he called to say sorry?

5 never / find
But for Patrizia, we _____
the stadium. We'd still be wandering the streets.

6 probably / be
If she'd stayed in her last job, she
_____ successful by now.

7 not / go
He regretted _____
to university when he had the chance to.

8 think
Of course that's what we should do. If only we
_____ of it before!

9 realise / you / already / do
I wouldn't have booked tickets for the concert if I
_____ it.

10 never / have
It's hard to imagine what life would have been like
if we _____ children.

GRAMMAR VERB PATTERNS

8 Complete the text with the correct form of the verbs in brackets.

¹_____ (talk) about loneliness is no problem for Aung San Suu Kyi. ²_____ (spend) more than fifteen years under house arrest in Burma, she is used to ³_____ (be) on her own. But loneliness doesn't seem ⁴_____ (be) one of the things that worried her. She says it's simply a matter of character. She is happy ⁵_____ (spend) time alone thinking, reading, listening to the radio and playing the piano, albeit badly.

After ⁶_____ (return) to Burma from the UK in 1988 ⁷_____ (look after) her dying mother, Aung San Suu Kyi responded to popular calls for her ⁸_____ (lead) the National League for Democracy. Despite the party ⁹_____ (win) a landslide victory in 1990, the military junta refused ¹⁰_____ (hand over) power and placed her under house arrest.

During that time, she was not able to see her two sons for many years or ¹¹_____ (visit) her sick husband when he was dying, for fear of ¹²_____ (not allow) back into the country. Regarded around the world as a hero for our times, Aung San Suu Kyi is renowned for her clarity of opinion and dedication to the people of her country.

VOCABULARY PLUS METAPHORS

9 Cross out the extra word in each sentence.

1 You've done really well, kid. You'll go too far.
2 It started off well, but quickly went downhill bottom from there.
3 Thanks for those comments. It's given us some food for the thought.
4 It was very shocking news. I found it hard for to swallow at first.
5 It's no good wasting precious all time worrying about things you can't change.
6 After all this time, I can't believe that they've come up with such a half-baked for idea.
7 I think he's reached for the peak of his career.
8 I found myself at a crossroads decision and wasn't sure what to do.
9 We'll need to put off aside some time to discuss this at the end of the meeting.
10 You just can't afford to spend so much time to watching television.
11 He has an incredible memory – he is forever regurgitating on obscure facts about things he has learnt.
12 We knew we would have to move out of the house, so it felt like we were forever living on borrowed money time.

FUNCTION INTRODUCING OPINIONS

10A Put the underlined words in the correct order to complete the sentences.

a) way / at / it / this / look: I have no option but to trust him.
b) far / I'm / as / concerned / as, there is simply no competition.
c) what / gather / from / can / I, this is the best route to take.
d) honest / you / my / opinion / want / if, I think you should take up the offer.
e) you / if / me / ask, it's a complete waste of time.
f) reality / the / is, I think you could get it cheaper elsewhere.

B Complete the conversations with the sentences in Exercise 10A.

1 A: I'm thinking of signing up for that course you did last month. Did you think it was worth it?
   B: _____
2 A: Do you really think that you can rely on Jim to keep this quiet?
   B: _____
3 A: I've been offered a promotion but I'm not sure I really want it. What do you think?
   B: _____
4 A: It's a lovely coat but I'm really not sure I can afford it.
   B: _____
5 A: Are you certain this is the best way to go?
   B: _____
6 A: What about all the other companies selling similar products?
   B: _____

CHECK

Circle the correct option to complete the sentences.

1 My mother's _____ name, before she married, was Karadia.
   a) married   **b)** maiden   **c)** single

2 She has had to work hard to _____ her name after the accusations.
   a) clean   **b)** repair   **c)** clear

3 We're planning on getting our own place but, for the moment, _____ with friends.
   a) we're staying   **b)** we stay   **c)** we'll be stayed

4 I can't believe how long I _____ for someone to take my call. I'm just listening to music.
   a) 've been waited   **b)** 've been waiting   **c)** wait

5 Excuse me, _____ to you?
   a) is this pen belonging   **b)** does this pen belonged
   c) does this pen belong

6 I'm _____ to take a romantic view of things.
   a) prone   **b)** tend   **c)** forever

7 As _____, I like to be in charge of these matters myself.
   a) an inclination   **b)** a tendency   **c)** a rule

8 My family have a _____ to exaggerate.
   a) tend   **b)** tendency   **c)** prone

9 She noticed lots of unexpected things and made some very _____ comments.
   a) apathetic   **b)** obstinate   **c)** perceptive

10 Small children are forever asking questions. They have such _____ minds.
   a) rebellious   **b)** inquisitive   **c)** over-ambitious

11 My father is eighty-six and he's very _____ in his ways.
   a) fixed   **b)** set   **c)** settled

12 She's a lovely girl but she's an incredible _____.
   a) black sheep   **b)** whizzkid   **c)** chatterbox

13 I _____ they must be in their seventies, wouldn't you say?
   a) suppose   **b)** say   **c)** hazard

14 She _____ to me to be happy with the situation.
   a) supposes   **b)** seems   **c)** says

15 I'd _____ a guess that there are problems in the relationship.
   a) reckon   **b)** wonder   **c)** hazard

16 If you can figure _____ a solution to this problem, I'll be very impressed.
   a) in   **b)** of   **c)** out

17 You must trust your _____ in business.
   a) instincts   **b)** qualification   **c)** feeling

18 _____ how strongly they would react, I simply wouldn't have told them.
   a) Had I known   **b)** Did I know   **c)** I had known

19 I wish I _____ earlier what was going on, then I might have been able to do something about it.
   a) would have realised   **b)** didn't realise
   c) 'd realised

20 If he hadn't experienced so many problems in the early stages, he _____.
   a) might have won   **b)** won   **c)** would win

21 I wanted to confront him about the issue but then I had _____ thoughts.
   a) first   **b)** second   **c)** third

22 I think the problem is that the managers can be very _____.
   a) perspective   **b)** stereotype   **c)** narrow-minded

23 _____ to appear stupid, he kept quiet.
   a) Not wanting   **b)** Not have wanted
   c) He was wanting not

24 Sam was always _____ by the other children.
   a) be picked on   **b)** being picked on
   c) been picked on

25 They were thought _____ by the back door.
   a) of having escaped   **b)** to have escaped
   c) to have escaping

26 I'm going to play devil's _____ here and say that I don't see why not.
   a) advocate   **b)** friend   **c)** partner

27 You were absolutely right to speak your _____.
   a) words   **b)** ideas   **c)** mind

28 As far as I _____, they can do what they like.
   a) concern   **b)** 'm concerned   **c)** 'm concerning

29 Look at it this _____, we all stand to lose.
   a) way   **b)** direction   **c)** how

30 From what I _____, there isn't a better solution.
   a) do see   **b)** can gather   **c)** should see

RESULT   /30

3) PLACES

VOCABULARY
LANDSCAPES

1 Underline the correct alternative.

1 It was a very *picturesque/bustling* place to sit, outside the restaurant on the quiet banks of the river.

2 The nightclub is in a rather *unspoilt/run-down* inner-city area.

3 The streets were *tranquil/bustling* with people.

4 We wandered around the beautiful, *run-down/ancient* walled city trying to imagine what life must have been like in those days.

5 The beaches there are completely *deserted/unspoilt* by tourism. It's wonderful.

6 The architecture was simply *picturesque/magnificent*. It was designed to impress.

7 The old mine now stands completely *ancient/deserted*. Nobody has worked there for nearly fifty years.

8 We love the Tuscan countryside. It's a beautifully *tranquil/run-down* place to be.

GRAMMAR
NOUN PHRASES

2 Complete the first paragraph of the brochure with phrases a)–g) and the second paragraph with phrases h)–n).

Paragraph 1

a) stunning landscape
b) before the main tourist season
c) the Aegean light reflecting off the blue and white-washed architecture
d) a series of cataclysmic volcanic eruptions
e) a two-week break
f) a thousand other eager tourists
g) spectacular sunsets the island is famous for

Paragraph 2

h) dense, more traditionally Islamic downtown area
i) a day trip to Petra
j) well-organised city
k) many Roman ruins that sprinkle the city
l) everyone, whatever their tastes
m) mesmerising city carved into the rock at Wadi Musa
n) slick suburbs to the west, lined with cafés and art galleries

 **Easy** trips

Why not visit Santorini, Greece, for ¹_____?
Santorini's ²_____ was sculpted by ³_____.
Come and enjoy the ⁴_____. It pays to visit
⁵_____, when you can watch ⁶_____ without
having to battle with ⁷_____ keen to enjoy the scene.

Or take a trip to the ⁸_____ of Amman, Jordan, where
old meets new. Split between ⁹_____, and the
¹⁰_____, Amman has something to offer ¹¹_____.

Maybe you could take ¹²_____, the ¹³_____, or
visit some of the ¹⁴_____.

LISTENING

3 A ▶ 3.1 Listen to the guide to Paris. Which of the topics in the box does the speaker mention?

terraced cafés   the smell of bread   theatre culture
busy restaurants   cobbled streets   clichés
designer handbags   famous department stores
poodles   the Eiffel Tower   the Pompidou Centre
flea markets   French wine   velib bikes

B Listen again. Are the statements true (T) or false (F)?

1 The terraced cafés are an important part of the flavour of Paris.
2 Paris does not have as much style as you would expect.
3 It's a wonderfully romantic city to spend time in.
4 Paris is not at all like you would expect from the clichés you hear.
5 It's not worth visiting the classic sights like the Eiffel Tower because there are too many tourists.
6 The real beauty of Paris is often hidden from the view of the tourist.
7 It's a good idea to hire a velib bike and cycle round the streets of Paris, like a Parisian would.
8 There is a lot to do in Paris, but you shouldn't try to do too much. Take your time to enjoy the city.

WRITING

A DESCRIPTION OF A PLACE; LEARN TO ADD DETAIL

4 A Read the travel review and answer the questions.

1 Where is the writer describing?
2 What is a good time to visit the area? Why?
3 How does the writer describe the landscape?
4 What kind of food does he mention?
5 What is the best way to get to Blidö?
6 What does the writer say about the atmosphere of the place? What contributes to that atmosphere?

B Underline other examples of detailed descriptions, particularly those involving the senses, that add colour to the writing.

C Write a description of a place you have visited (200–250 words). Use the text in Exercise 4A as a model and include some of the following:

- Introduction/location
- How to get there
- Landscape/flora/fauna/atmosphere
- Food/drink/activities
- Description of a typical scene
- Particular recommendations

Here comes the sun:
A midsummer's trip to the Swedish island of Blidö

The Stockholm archipelago consists of over 24,000 islands and islets scattered across the Baltic Sea. The nearest to the shore are divided by causeways from the mainland and possess all the amenities of modern Sweden. Other islands are served by free and efficient public ferries. The outer islands are reachable only by private boat. The rule of thumb is that the further out, the greater the isolation. First plumbing, then electricity disappears until finally, out in the Baltic Sea, tiny huts share a few metres of exposed granite with just the wind and seals.

The archipelago is a place of beauty at any time, but during Midsummer, it's the place to be. On the way out to the archipelago from Stockholm, the road winds through the radiant green landscape of a fairytale – forests, timber houses, rye fields, fat cows. Wild flowers nod in the hedgerows. Road signs warn of rogue moose.

In Norrtälje, the gateway town to the archipelago, the supermarket is packed with trolleys the day before Midsummer's Eve. The prescribed Midsummer foods of strawberries, herring, new potatoes and sour cream are flying off the shelves. A worker complains that they're shifting a tonne of potatoes every hour. Heavily laden cars leave the car park for the islands.

For my inaugural Midsummer Eve, I'm heading to the island of Blidö. It's not remote – just two short ferry trips to cross the bay – but the pace of life soon slows. The air is luminously clear and, scoured by sea breezes, feels like it's rejuvenating the lungs. Roe deer skip out of the path of bicycles on the roads.

Adapted from Lonely Planet Magazine (May 2011)

READING

1 A Read the article and match statements 1–14 with people a)–f).

1 His workspace was large.
2 His desk was technology-free.
3 He ignored his own advice.
4 He worked in bed.
5 He had living creatures in his workspace.
6 He worked with chaos around him.
7 He made art out of things in his studio.
8 His workspace was not especially exciting.
9 His studio is on display.
10 He displayed his work in his studio.
11 There is something strange about the furniture in his room.
12 He had expensive things in his workspace.
13 He had a teaching tool in his workspace.
14 His workspace was not dark.

a) Francis Bacon
b) Henri Matisse
c) Pablo Picasso
d) Albert Einstein
e) Ernest Hemingway
f) Woody Allen

B Circle the correct definition.

1 jutting (paragraph 1)
  a) making bright colours   b) sticking out
2 precariously (paragraph 1)
  a) beautifully   b) likely to fall
3 spare (paragraph 2)
  a) full of objects   b) basic, with nothing unnecessary
4 spark off (paragraph 2)
  a) cause   b) destroy
5 opulent (paragraph 3)
  a) with expensive decoration   b) with a good smell
6 doodles (paragraph 3)
  a) large, completed paintings   b) unplanned drawings
7 scrawled (paragraph 4)
  a) written with great care   b) written carelessly
8 humble (paragraph 5)
  a) modest   b) large

VOCABULARY

-Y ADJECTIVES

2 Underline the correct alternative.

1 It was a dark, *poky/jokey/gaudy* room with a broken door and no windows.
2 This room is too *gaudy/chilly/fiery* for my taste. The colours are too bright.
3 The house is really *shady/roomy/spacy*. There's lots of space.
4 The town is very *roomy/weary/dreary*. All the buildings are grey and there's nothing to do.
5 This flat is nice and *poky/brightly/airy* with big windows.
6 Come and sit under this *airy/shadowy/shady* tree and talk to me.
7 It's quite *gaudy/chilly/airy* in here. Can you close the window, please?
8 The weather's looking a bit *roomy/shady/gloomy*. I think it's going to rain.

 # Room for a genius?

The English painter Francis Bacon may not have been the greatest artist in history but he was certainly the messiest. His London studio is a bombed-out catastrophe of paintbrushes jutting out of jars and cans, mouldering champagne boxes, books balanced precariously in irregular towers and photos lying on every surface. After his death in 1992, his entire studio – the walls, floorboards, boxes, drops of paint, dust, everything – was transplanted to an art gallery in Ireland. The studio itself had become a modernist masterpiece, a perfect example of the relationship between genius and chaos. Bacon once wrote that he couldn't paint in tidy rooms. Few would argue with that. It took a team of ten archaeologists and conservators three years to move and reassemble the mess.

What types of work area do other creative geniuses need? Should the room be a spare, minimalist shell to allow space for the mind to wander? Or should it be cluttered with the objects of everyday life to spark off ideas and inspiration? Is big better than small? What of the light? Should the room be bursting with sunbeams or so dark and cramped that it forces the imagination to fly?

The French painter Henri Matisse worked in a famously opulent studio. The high ceilings led the eye down to his paintings, which were perfectly arranged on the walls, and the room contained elaborate tapestries, vases, sculptures, potted plants, doves in a cage. His near-contemporary Pablo Picasso had an altogether different style. His studio was packed full of his own creations – little pots and clay figures, scribbles and doodles, and all kinds of junk that he would later assemble into masterpieces – lumps of iron, fragments of glass, animal bones.

Another genius of Matisse's era, Albert Einstein, kept his office full of books and paper. His desk was spectacularly cluttered with no space for a typewriter or telephone. Behind his chair was a simple blackboard with mathematical equations scrawled in white chalk. Einstein once said, 'A table, a chair, a bowl of fruit and a violin; what else does a man need to be happy?' The answer, judging by his office, is a pile of paper.

Ernest Hemingway's workspace in his Florida home was relatively humble: a few bookshelves, large windows to let in the light and a tall desk made of dark wood. One thing looks wrong; the chair is too small for the table. The reason for this is that he didn't actually use the chair for working. For much of his life, Hemingway wrote standing up (he ignored his own first 'rule' for aspiring writers: 'apply the seat of the pants to the seat of the chair'). Writing masterpieces while standing up might sound strange but maybe not as odd as the working habits of Mark Twain, Marcel Proust and Woody Allen. All of them wrote in bed.

GRAMMAR
RELATIVE CLAUSES

3 Choose the correct options to complete the text.

Hotel crawler

When Dutchman Vincent van Dijk ¹_____ as a lifestyle trend watcher, moved to Amsterdam for his job, he couldn't find a place to live.

He'd been staying in hotels for several weeks, ²_____ he hit on a great idea. Carrying nothing but the suitcase ³_____ all his possessions were contained, he decided to stay in a different hotel every night for a year and blog about his experiences. He realised that through his blogging, each hotel ⁴_____ he was staying could gain valuable publicity, so he began asking the managers if he could stay for free in exchange for a write-up in his blog. Most of the managers ⁵_____ hotels were struggling in the wake of the financial crisis, were delighted with the idea.

The hotels ⁶_____ he wrote varied from cheap hostels to five-star luxury spots. Some hotel managers treated him like a king, greeting him personally on arrival, preparing the finest suite on offer or letting him dine for free. He luxuriated in a €3,500-a-night room ⁷_____ it took him ten minutes to switch off all the lights (he joked in his blog). Another room had an en suite bathroom ⁸_____ would not be out of place in a royal palace. But he also stayed in cheap dives, ⁹_____ were barely habitable. He came across hotels that smelt of fresh paint and cigarette smoke, a room ¹⁰_____ was no wider than a toilet, and curtains covering crumbling walls.

Vincent van Dijk's idea was an audacious project, but probably only do-able by someone ¹¹_____ hotels are one of life's great pleasures. Despite offers from hotels in London, Paris and Rio, van Dijk stayed put in Holland ¹²_____ he plans to write a book about Amsterdam's accommodation.

1 a) , who works   b) who works   c) that works
2 a) was when   b) at which point   c) which point
3 a) which in   b) which   c) in which
4 a) that   b) where   c) which
5 a) whom   b) whose   c) , whose
6 a) , about which   b) that   c) about which
7 a) in which   b) which   c) in where
8 a) that   b) at which   c) , that
9 a) which some   b) some which   c) some of which
10 a) that   b) where there   c) in which it
11 a) who   b) for whom   c) for which
12 a) where   b) , where   c) on which

VOCABULARY PLUS
PREFIXES

4 Complete the text with the prefixes in the box.

anti- de- im- ir- mal- mis- non-
over- post- pre- pro- un- under-

REBUILDING NEW ORLEANS

When Hurricane Katrina hit New Orleans in August 2005, to say the city was ¹_____ prepared would be an ²_____ statement. The flood that followed the hurricane was completely ³_____powering. Clubs, bars, restaurants and homes went under. Eighty percent of the city's buildings were flooded.

But it wasn't just the weather that contributed to the disaster; politics was involved. Many people, regardless of whether they were ⁴_____-government or ⁵_____-government, thought the crisis in New Orleans was ⁶_____managed – the response from the federal authorities seemed far too slow. A ⁷_____-mortem on the city would have said 'completely devastated, but not entirely due to natural causes'.

Such was the damage that when the rebuilding eventually started, the job looked like mission ⁸_____possible. Gradually, however, New Orleans got back on its feet. The residents returned to fix up the buildings. Several ⁹_____-profit organisations contributed time and money and some celebrities, such as George Clooney and Steven Spielberg, sent big cheques. Old neighbourhoods came back to life and the ¹⁰_____functioning city began to function again.

Although many residents returned, the city is still ¹¹_____populated, with about 70 percent of its ¹²_____-Katrina population living there. What has returned, though, is the city's vibrancy. The musicians are back on the streets, several movies and TV shows are being filmed there and some famous local hangouts like The Cat's Meow and Bourbon Street Blues have reopened.

Local entrepreneur Davide Marchionise says, 'The damage was terrible, but not ¹³_____reversible. Look around the city. It's still the biggest party in the country.'

VOCABULARY

CITY LIFE

1 Complete the crossword.

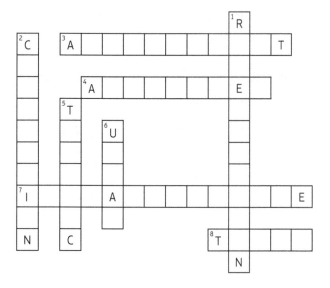

Across

3 when buildings are left to fall apart, with no one living in or using them

4 basic things that we need, e.g. running water and electricity

7 the internal systems of a country or city, e.g. roads and railways

8 fees charged for using certain roads or bridges

Down

1   see 6

2   see 5

5, 2   when the roads are blocked with too many cars (two words)

6, 1   the rebuilding and modernisation of parts of a city (two words)

FUNCTION

MAKING A PROPOSAL

2 A Read the proposal and change one word in each sentence to improve the speech. Change ten words in total.

Proposal for a cultural centre

To start with, I'm going to talk brief about the beginnings of the project. Just to give a bit of backing information, we first discussed the idea of a cultural centre two years ago. The ambition of the project is to create a space for people to see art, listen to music and watch films together. So the main desire of our proposal is to provide a community resource. The long-term blessings include bringing the community together and promoting the arts.

What we arrange to do is work with local companies to involve them in all areas of the project – design, construction, maintenance and services. While cost is a major issue, our resolution is to ask local government for grant money. In the first instant, this would mean putting together our budget plan and after that, we would write a grant application.

To close up, we feel this is a very worthwhile project for our community. Are there any questions or things that need clearing?

B ▶ 3.2 Listen and check.

LEARN TO

SUGGEST MODIFICATIONS

3 Put B's words in the correct order to make responses.

1 A: They want to do this and we want to do that.
   B: our / about / we / how / ideas / combine / if / ?

_____

2 A: So, as I see it, we have a dilemma.
   B: at / it / look / way / another / let's

_____

3 A: Those are our two options. Does anyone have any other ideas?
   B: compromise / I'd / propose / to / a / like

_____

4 A: The project is going to be very expensive.
   B: can / there / any / costs / reduce / way / the / is / we / ?

_____

5 A: It's going to be difficult to finish on time.
   B: regarding / any / there / schedule / leeway / is / the

_____

6 A: So, to summarise, this is a tricky problem.
   B: with / try / let's / solution / to / up / a / come

_____

VOCABULARY

CRIME COLLOCATIONS

1 Complete the sentences with the words in the box.

> convictions   crime   drug-related   innocence
> raid   report   suspend   wrongful

1 The judge's decision was to _____ the sentence to reflect the accused's previous good character.

2 To keep her identity secret, the witness used a public phone box to _____ the crime.

3 Three businessmen facing a life sentence for fraud protested their _____.

4 The press knew in advance about the dawn _____.

5 New evidence has proved that the original trial resulted in a _____ conviction.

6 If you commit a _____, you must be prepared to take the consequences.

7 An international gang has been arrested at the airport and charged with a _____ offence.

8 The government has decided that in some cases, the jury may be made aware of a defendant's previous _____ or charges.

GRAMMAR

INTRODUCTORY IT

2 Add *it* or *it's* to B's part of the conversations where necessary.

1 A: You seem on edge. Is there something bothering you?
   B: No, nothing really. Just that I'm worried about my interview tomorrow.

2 A: Do you have the time on you?
   B: Yes, about nine forty.

3 A: Are you having trouble with that?
   B: Yes, I find really hard to close the safe once I've opened it.

4 A: Have you tried Javier's number?
   B: Pointless calling him now. Too late.

5 A: Is there anything else you need me to do?
   B: Yes, I'd really appreciate if you could lock up when you go.

6 A: I'm absolutely exhausted.
   B: No wonder you're tired. You hardly slept last night.

7 A: Have you had a chance to visit Loch Lomond?
   B: No, but I've heard that a wonderful place for walking holidays.

8 A: Have you thought about which restaurant would be best for the meeting?
   B: No, I'll leave to you to decide which one is most suitable.

3 Complete the sentences with the words in the box.

> hard   appear   appreciate   wonder
> pointless   help   fault   amazes

1 It's _____ to know if we've done the right thing or not.

2 Don't blame Sam. It's not his _____ if he can't sing.

3 I can't _____ it if I'm lucky.

4 It would _____ that the attacker escaped through the back door.

5 It always _____ me how beautiful the sky is at this time of year.

6 It's no _____ you can't see – you've got the wrong glasses on!

7 It's _____ trying to contact him now – he won't have his phone switched on.

8 I'd _____ it if you didn't tell anyone about this conversation.

4 Complete the second sentence with two to six words so that it has a similar meaning to the first.

1 The station is a long way from here.
   It's _____ _____ _____ _____ _____ _____ from here.

2 We bump into each other amazingly often.
   It's _____ _____ _____ _____ _____ _____ each other.

3 I think we're too late.
   It seems _____ _____ _____ _____ late.

4 Somebody suggested that they reopen the inquiry.
   It was _____ _____ _____ _____ be reopened.

5 It was hard for me to believe he gave me his autograph.
   I couldn't _____ _____ _____ _____ _____ _____ his autograph.

6 People letting me down is something I don't like.
   I hate _____ _____ _____ _____ me down.

7 I think he deserves to be told the truth.
   We owe _____ _____ _____ to tell him the truth.

8 I'm not sure if we've done the right thing.
   It's hard _____ _____ if we've done the right thing.

9 Getting on with people is not difficult for me.
   I find _____ _____ _____ _____ _____ with people.

10 I think you should decide what the best way to deal with this is.
   I'll leave _____ _____ _____ _____ _____ the best way to deal with this.

VOCABULARY PLUS

LEXICAL CHUNKS

5 Complete the text with the lexical chunks in the box. You don't need to use all the phrases.

> at that time miscarriage of justice demanded justice
> a surprising number of people unjustly accused rough justice
> protested his innocence the true story of crime committed

Wrongly convicted

Cinema loves a miscarriage of justice story. Whether purely fictional or based on genuine events, the innocent man who is ¹_____ appeals to ²_____, creating some of the best-known cinematic classics, such as Alfred Hitchcock's *The Wrong Man* or Jim Sheridan's ground-breaking *In the Name of the Father*.

Although Hitchcock generally preferred to work with fictional stories, *The Wrong Man* was inspired by ³_____ Christopher Emmanuel Balestrero, whose life fell apart after he was wrongly sentenced to life imprisonment for armed robbery, although he strongly ⁴_____ throughout.

HAVE YOU SEEN The Wrong Man
--ALFRED HITCHCOCK'S NEWEST ADVENTURE INTO TERROR!
HENRY FONDA · VERA MILES in ALFRED HITCHCOCK'S THE WRONG MAN

In the Name of the Father is arguably one of the most high-impact ⁵_____ stories ever. Based on the book *Proved Innocent,* the film tells the story of the Guildford Four – four young men who were wrongly imprisoned for the 1974 bombing of two pubs in Guildford and Woolwich, in the UK. During their sentence, the men endured ⁶_____ within the prison system. They later ⁷_____ for the way they had been treated and for their years of false imprisonment, thus exposing the judicial and police malpractice which they had encountered ⁸_____.

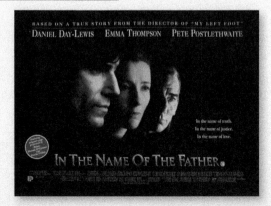

DANIEL DAY-LEWIS · EMMA THOMPSON · PETE POSTLETHWAITE
IN THE NAME OF THE FATHER

LISTENING

6 A ▶ 4.1 Listen to the story of Henry Roberts. Complete the summary.

> Henry Roberts was convicted of a crime he
> ¹_____.
> He spent ²_____
> in jail. The man who was actually guilty of the crime later ³_____.

B Listen again and circle the correct answers.

1 What crime was Henry Roberts accused of?
 a) theft
 b) murder
 c) fraud

2 When did the murder take place?
 a) five years ago
 b) more than ten years ago
 c) more than twenty years ago

3 How long was Roberts sent to prison for?
 a) five years
 b) fifteen years
 c) fifty years

4 What was the relationship between the man who died and Henry Roberts?
 a) He was his nephew.
 b) He was his uncle.
 c) He was his friend.

5 Was Henry Roberts shot during the incident?
 a) Yes, he was.
 b) No, he wasn't.
 c) We don't know.

6 What happened to the murder weapon?
 a) It was left at the scene.
 b) It was never found.
 c) It was thrown into a river.

7 Why were the statements taken from Henry Roberts unreliable?
 a) He was under medication when he made them.
 b) He was a habitual liar.
 c) Nobody witnessed the shooting.

8 What evidence did the police fail to follow up on?
 a) DNA evidence
 b) an anonymous phone call
 c) eye-witness statements

GRAMMAR
THE PERFECT ASPECT

1 Match 1–8, a)–h) and i)–viii) to make complete sentences.

1	I've been	**a)**	hasn't spoken
2	None of us	**b)**	because I'd
3	That girl	**c)**	been working here
4	I felt happy	**d)**	living in the
5	When I saw her,	**e)**	she'd been
6	We will	**f)**	seems to have
7	The house	**g)**	had ever heard
8	They'll have	**h)**	probably have

i) to her mother for over ten years.

ii) running and was out of breath.

iii) got smaller since I moved out of it!

iv) same flat since I was eighteen.

v) been to Asia this time next year.

vi) for six years in May.

vii) of that actor before we saw the film.

viii) just passed my exam.

2 Complete the sentences with the correct perfect form of the verbs in brackets.

1 When they found Chris, he said he _____ (live) on the streets for years.

2 I _____ (not finish) the project by Monday. I still have to do all the research.

3 Sorry about the delay. _____ (wait) long?

4 Before he died he told us he _____ (bury) the money in the garden.

5 We asked the neighbours, but they seem _____ (not notice) anything strange.

6 I hear you're looking for a job. Who _____ (speak to) so far?

7 By 2020, Martha _____ (work) for the same company for fifty years.

8 Seeing Liz after twenty years, I realised she _____ (not change) at all.

VOCABULARY
SOCIAL ISSUES

3 A Match the quotations with the issues in the box.

child labour   economic development   gun control
free trade   intellectual property   capital punishment
freedom of speech   environmental awareness
illegal immigration   civil liberties

1 You can cage the singer but not the song. (Harry Belafonte)

2 No man is above the law and no man is below it. (Theodore Roosevelt)

3 To take a life when a life has been lost is revenge, not justice. (Desmond Tutu)

4 I did something that challenged the banking world. Conventional banks look for the rich; we look for the absolutely poor. All people are entrepreneurs, but many don't have the opportunity to find that out. (Muhammad Yunus)

5 There's no copyright on ideas. They fly on the wind. (Marilisa Jauregui)

6 Why do we have to pay the price of poverty? We didn't create poverty; adults did. (Sultana, 12, Bangladesh)

7 For target shooting, that's OK. Get a license and go to the range. For defence of the home, that's why we have police departments. (James Brady)

8 Most of the US's problems stem from the fact that the Native Americans didn't have very good border controls five hundred years ago. (Nikola Hertosch)

9 The more we exploit nature, the more our options are reduced until we have only one: to fight for survival. (Morris K. Udall)

10 The most important single central fact about a free market is that no exchange takes place unless both parties benefit. (Milton Friedman)

B ▶ **4.2** Listen to the answers and mark the stress in each phrase.

C Listen again and repeat. Focus on the correct stress.

WRITING
A PROBLEM-SOLUTION ESSAY; LEARN TO USE PARALLELISM

4 A Read the introductions from three essays about social problems. How can parallelism improve each paragraph? Rewrite the sentences that need editing using parallelism. The first one has been done for you.

1 Throughout the world, over 150 million children aged 5–14 work regularly. Many find themselves in dangerous conditions. These include working in places with no sanitation, working in mines, being employed to work *working* with unsafe machinery or having a job *working* in a heavily polluted atmosphere.

2 The internet does many wonderful things – it brings people closer together, it promotes new forms of creativity, entertainment is provided on the internet and the internet allows us to access information quickly. One thing it does not do well is protect people's rights to their intellectual property.

3 The world's most industrialised countries are using up the planet's resources. We drive too many gas-guzzling cars, recycle too little, find that we are producing too much waste from packaging and too much of our food is thrown away. Some simple habits can change our lifestyles for the better and can also help to save the environment.

B Complete one of the essays above. Write about 250 words.

READING

5 A What is the connection between the man and the flag? Read to find out.

The unknown hero

1 On June 24th, 1859, thirty-one-year-old Henri Dunant, from Switzerland, travelled to Solferino, northern Italy, intending to discuss his failing business interests with Napoleon III. Instead of tea and cakes with the Emperor, he got the shock of his life. Dunant arrived just in time to see the aftermath of the Battle of Solferino, a nine-hour bloodbath that left tens of thousands dead and wounded, strewn across 15 kilometres of Italian countryside; he would later describe the scene as 'chaotic disorder, despair unspeakable and misery of every kind'. The French army had fewer doctors than vets – horses were more valuable in war than men – so, abandoning his plans to meet Napoleon, Dunant set about mobilising local people to help care for the wounded. At his insistence, the volunteers did not discriminate according to the colour of the soldiers' uniforms; medical care was given to all. From this principle arose the organisation that Dunant helped to found four years later – the International Committee of the Red Cross.

2 Dunant was an unlikely hero. Born in Geneva, he was a poor student who went on to become an even worse businessman. Even during the early days of the Red Cross, he had to resign from the committee. His businesses were collapsing all around him and the authorities had ordered his arrest. He fled Geneva, never to return. In the next twenty years, he went from country to country, part-fugitive, part-businessman, part-mouthpiece for the Red Cross. He once fainted while giving a speech in Plymouth, UK. Apparently, he hadn't eaten for days.

3 He eventually returned to Switzerland and settled in a small town called Heiden. Six years later, he became the first recipient of the Nobel Peace Prize. The citation for the award said, 'Without you, the Red Cross, the supreme humanitarian achievement of the nineteenth century, would probably have never been undertaken'. He asked that the prize money be administered from Norway so that none of his creditors could get their hands on it.

4 Today, the International Red Cross and Red Crescent Movement has almost 100 million members, who operate all over the world. Its emblem, the inverse of Switzerland's national flag, is an international symbol of humanitarian grace.

5 If his organisation is a giant force for good, Henri Dunant himself is barely remembered. A small museum in Heiden remains infrequently visited (the people of Heiden didn't like him much – he refused to speak German) and his name is not universally known. Before he died at the age of eighty-two, he stated that he wished to be buried in Zurich without a ceremony. But fate had the last laugh. In 1944, in the same Heiden hospital where Dunant had died thirty-four years previously, a baby was born. That baby was Jakob Kellenberger, who, in 1998, became president of the International Committee of the Red Cross.

B Read the text again. One sentence has been removed from each paragraph. Add sentences 1–5 to the correct place in the paragraphs.

1 There was little organised medical care.
2 Time and again he found himself fleeing his debts.
3 He withdrew from the world, but all this changed in 1895 when an article was written about the International Committee of the Red Cross.
4 From Dunant's early solo efforts, the organisation has grown steadily over the last 150 years.
5 His wish was granted.

C Are the statements about the text true (T) or false (F)?

1 Dunant took part in the Battle of Solferino.
2 Dunant discussed business with Napoleon III.
3 Dunant served on the committee of the Red Cross.
4 Dunant lived in many countries because he wanted his organisation to grow.
5 Dunant was well known until 1895.
6 The emblem of the Red Cross is the same as Switzerland's national flag.
7 Dunant did not want to be buried in Heiden or Geneva.
8 In the hospital where Dunant died, a future president of the Red Cross was born.

D Find words in the text to match definitions 1–8.

1 the period of time after something (e.g. war, storm) when people are still dealing with the results (paragraph 1)
_____
2 the violent killing of many people at one time (paragraph 1) _____
3 injured by a weapon such as a gun or a knife (paragraph 1) _____
4 scattered or thrown around a large area (paragraph 1) _____
5 someone who receives something (paragraph 3) _____
6 people, banks or companies that you owe money to (paragraph 3) _____
7 a picture, shape or object that is used to represent a country or organisation (paragraph 4) _____
8 the complete opposite of something (paragraph 4) _____

VOCABULARY

DECISIONS

1 Write one word in each gap to complete the letter and the Agony Aunt's response.

Dear Suki

Dear Suki,

I'm ¹_____ a tricky predicament. Four months ago a friend was fired from the company where we both worked. He is now doing consulting work for a rival company and I think he has started giving away our company's secrets. I'm now ²_____ with a dilemma. Do I confront him about this and risk losing our friendship or should I say nothing? I'm also trying to ³_____ up the pros and cons of telling my boss, but I can't decide. I have to ⁴_____ into consideration the fact that I have no proof against my friend.

Mel

Dear Mel,

You need to assess ⁵_____ situation from different viewpoints. Is your friend breaking the law? Might your boss already know what he's doing? How much secret information does he have? Bear in ⁶_____ the fact that companies have few real secrets these days. Employees tend to move a lot between companies and take some inside knowledge with them. So, before you do anything, think ⁷_____ through carefully. Without proof, is there any point in talking to your boss about it? Also consider the benefits and ⁸_____ of confronting your friend. What will he say? He'll either admit it, in which case your friendship is over, or he'll deny it, in which case your friendship is still over.

Suki, Agony Aunt

FUNCTION

EXPRESSING HYPOTHETICAL PREFERENCES

2 Cross out the extra word in seven of the sentences.
1 Without a shadow but of a doubt, I'd choose Johnny.
2 My preference would be to have a female president.
3 If it was for up to me, I'd never do that.
4 No right way would I do that.
5 I'd just as soon stay at home as travel.
6 Far the better to be a living coward than a brave corpse.
7 Given to the choice, I'd prefer to go by plane than train.
8 I'd sooner to live here than there.
9 This would be by very far the best option.
10 If I ever found myself in that situation, I wouldn't panic.

3 A Read the hypothetical situation below and think about what you would do.

You are in a hurry to catch a plane home after a long trip. You stop briefly to buy a present for your partner. While you are in the shop, you see someone shoplifting. If you report the theft, you will probably miss your plane. What do you do?

B ▶ 4.3 Listen to a man and woman discussing the situation. Who says the sentences below, the man (M) or the woman (W)? Three of the sentences are not used.
1 If I ever found myself in this situation, I'd probably just ignore it.
2 If it was up to me, I'd turn the shoplifter in to the police.
3 Given the choice, I'd just ignore it.
4 No way would I ignore it.
5 I'd just as soon tell the shopkeeper.
6 Without a shadow of a doubt I'd tell someone.
7 My preference would be just to alert someone to what's going on.
8 Far better to miss your plane.
9 This would be by far the best option.
10 I'd sooner do that than let the shoplifter get away with it.

LEARN TO

ADD EMPHASIS

4 A Circle the correct option to complete the conversations.
1 A: Smoking should be banned.
   B: I _____ agree.
   a) incredibly   b) completely   c) am
2 A: I think you should resign.
   B: That's out of the _____.
   a) possibility   b) order   c) question
3 A: Why are you leaving?
   B: The _____ is, I'm too old for this job.
   a) fact   b) way   c) certainty
4 A: Will you buy me that laptop?
   B: No _____.
   a) possibility   b) chance   c) chances
5 A: Why aren't you coming?
   B: The _____ is, I've had enough of parties.
   a) thought   b) idea   c) thing
6 A: Can I borrow your motorbike?
   B: Not _____ your life.
   a) on   b) by   c) for
7 A: I think mobile phones are a good learning tool.
   B: You're _____ right.
   a) really   b) incredibly   c) absolutely

B ▶ 4.4 Listen and check.

C Listen again and repeat B's sentences. Pay attention to the intonation.

GRAMMAR NOUN PHRASES

1 Add details to the sentences by using the information in brackets to make noun phrases. Pay attention to word order.

1 Bones have been found. (in a cave / several piles of / in Ethiopia / prehistoric)

Several piles of prehistoric bones have been found
in a cave in Ethiopia.

2 It was a necklace. (that he'd given her / diamond / 15-carat / with a gold chain)

_____

3 We moved to the town. (where we'd met / small / border / for the first time)

_____

4 They bought her a car. (worth £50,000 / sports / brand new / red)

_____

5 He got a tattoo. (multicoloured / on his arm / of his daughter / large)

_____

6 Jodie bought a cat. (grey / tiny / Siamese / with a white mark on its face)

_____

7 She married a teacher. (from Jordan / Science / charming / but based in France)

_____

8 Let's meet in the restaurant. (on the corner / Italian / same / where we ate mussels)

_____

VOCABULARY REVIEW I

2 In each description A–D the three underlined words are jumbled up. Swap them round so they are in the right place.

A The [1]congestion was just terrible. The transport system is especially bad so everyone drives everywhere, which leads to a lot of traffic [2]dreary. The downtown area is quite [3]infrastructure, too – just tall, grey office blocks.

B The landscape was very [4]deserted – snow-capped mountains and little streams. Despite its fame, the place is completely [5]picturesque and untouched by the tourist industry. In fact, it was [6]unspoilt; we didn't see anyone else for over an hour.

C We arrived in a very [7]airy area full of boarded-up buildings and dogs roaming the streets. Our hotel was very [8]run-down from the outside – barely lit, walls dark with dirt. But at least the rooms were [9]gloomy, with large, high windows and a view of the city.

D Our hotel was close to a [10]ancient market. It was great to wander around, though it got a bit [11]bustling in the evenings. The other nice thing is that the area is full of [12]chilly buildings, some dating from the fifteenth century.

GRAMMAR RELATIVE CLAUSES

3 Complete the second sentence so that it has a similar meaning to the first. Include the word given.

1 She's written two books, but I haven't read either of them.
NEITHER
She's written two books, _____
_____.

2 If your meeting is cancelled, you can come to lunch with me.
CASE
Your meeting may be cancelled, in _____
_____.

3 I spoke to six people and not one had heard of Justin Bieber.
NONE
I spoke to six people, _____
_____.

4 We should be grateful for the fact that no one was hurt in the accident.
WHICH
No one was hurt in the accident, _____
_____.

5 When he got out of the car, I realised he was famous.
POINT
He got out of the car, _____
_____.

6 The majority of the 50,000 people at the concert had been fans in the 60s.
MOST
There were 50,000 people at the concert,
_____
_____.

7 That man's books inspired me to become an anthropologist.
BOOKS
He's the writer _____
_____.

8 This is the hotel where that actor died.
IN
This is the hotel _____
_____.

9 We arrived at the airport at 6.00, but our plane had already left.
WHICH
We arrived at the airport at 6.00, by _____
_____.

10 My parents love dancing so they're going to do a tango course.
BOTH
My parents, _____
_____.

VOCABULARY PLUS PREFIXES

4 Complete B's responses with the words in the box plus the correct prefix.

> ~~attractive~~ behaves cooked criminalised
> historic moral nourished populated
> replaceable social

1 **A:** That house is so ugly.
   B: Yes, it is rather *unattractive* .
2 **A:** We'll never find another leader like Sami.
   B: Yes, he's absolutely _____ .
3 **A:** That child is completely out of control.
   B: I know. His parents do nothing when he _____ .
4 **A:** Lola hates talking to people.
   B: I know. She's very _____ .
5 **A:** What that banker did was very unethical.
   B: I agree. I thought it was completely _____ .
6 **A:** The city has far too many people.
   B: Yes, I'd heard it was _____ .
7 **A:** Many will starve because of the disaster.
   B: Over thirty percent of the children there are already _____ .
8 **A:** The meat tasted almost raw.
   B: Yes, I thought it was a bit _____ .
9 **A:** It's not illegal anymore.
   B: Yes, I heard it had been _____ .
10 **A:** These paintings were done before recorded time.
    B: So you're saying they're _____ ?

FUNCTION MAKING A PROPOSAL

5 Read the proposal. Some lines have an extra word. Tick the correct lines and write the extra words.

Just to give over some background information, the proposal	**1** _over_
is based on the Dutch town of Groningen, which has the	**2** ✓
highest percentage of bicycle use in the Europe.	**3** _____
To start with, I'm going to talk to briefly about the benefits of a	**4** _____
'cycling' city. The strong aim of the project is to reduce the	**5** _____
number of cars in the city centre.	**6** _____
The main and objective of our proposal is to improve the	**7** _____
environment while also providing economic and health boosts	**8** _____
for the population. What we are plan to do is create a car-free city	**9** _____
centre. We're going to build walkways, cycle lanes and a bus lane.	**10** _____
This solution will help us make the city a very better place to live.	**11** _____
In the first of instance, this would mean digging up the main roads.	**12** _____
The long-term of benefits include healthier lifestyles for citizens,	**13** _____
less pollution and an end to traffic congestion. So, basically, what	**14** _____
we're for proposing is to completely change our town.	**15** _____
Is there anything that needs the clarification?	**16** _____

VOCABULARY REVIEW 2

6 Join words from boxes A and B and use them to complete the sentences.

> **A** intellectual illegal drugs previous
> appeal child freedom economic
> environmental driving gun capital

> **B** punishment offence immigration
> of speech raid against property
> convictions control labour
> awareness development

1 By copying my essay, they stole my _____ .
2 You cannot silence someone if your country has _____ .
3 I had _____ for burglary and theft, but I was innocent.
4 The lawyer advised her to _____ her sentence as it was particularly harsh.
5 For that kind of crime, I think _____ is suitable.
6 We need stricter _____ laws to prevent criminals from buying weapons.
7 The _____ resulted in several arrests and the destruction of a cannabis farm.
8 A _____, for example, speeding, doesn't usually result in a prison sentence.
9 With the increase in pollution, _____ becomes even more important.
10 Boys and girls as young as five are involved in _____ .
11 Even if you close the border, it won't stop _____ .
12 The _____ of poor countries will be helped by this trade agreement.

GRAMMAR INTRODUCTORY IT

7 Complete the text with the phrases in the box.

> find it impossible   it always amazes
> it appears that   it's believed that the
> it's no   it's pointless   it will be easier
> love it   make it clear   it makes

¹_____ thieves don't like pink. Reacting to a recent increase in petty theft from gardens, police are advising people to paint their garden tools pink.
²_____ 'Paint it Pink' project will be successful for two reasons: firstly, ³_____ to identify the stolen goods and secondly, ⁴_____ the re-selling of the stolen items more difficult because few buyers want pink tools. As everyone knows, ⁵_____ trying to retrieve, say, a black metal spade. There are millions of them. But a pink one is different. Gardener Rod Hampson says,
'⁶_____ me when people leave their tools lying around in the garden. ⁷_____ wonder crime is rising. Thieves ⁸_____ when they can just jump over a fence and grab something. But they'd ⁹_____ to sell a bright pink tool.'
The police want to ¹⁰_____ that people should also use padlocks and sheds, but that 'Paint it Pink' is an additional measure.

VOCABULARY PLUS LEXICAL CHUNKS

8 A Match 1–5 with a)–e) to make complete sentences.

1 Disgraced politician Mary Klein escaped
2 He decided to take the law into
3 Children practise rough
4 When it comes to catching the bad guys, it's up
5 It was the sheriff's job to uphold

a) justice by <u>fleeing the country</u>.
b) to the police to get the job done.
c) justice on each other every day of the week.
d) justice, but he was past retirement age.
e) his own hands when he realised he had no choice.

B Underline the lexical chunks in a)–e). The first one has been done for you.

GRAMMAR THE PERFECT ASPECT

9 Underline the correct alternatives.

A valuable collection of film posters ¹*has been discovered/ had been discovered* in the walls of a Victorian home. Last week, just days after Joseph Winkleman ²*has bought/had bought* the house, a storm hit and rain poured through the roof, damaging the walls. Winkleman ³*has been planning/had been planning* to reconstruct the walls, but the storm meant he started immediately. As workers tore down the plaster, they found thousands of old film posters. Previously, the house ⁴*had been belonging/had belonged* to the son of a man who had been the manager of a local cinema during the 1920s and 30s and was thought ⁵*to have been/to had been* wealthy. It turns out that for twenty years, the cinema manager ⁶*had brought/had been bringing* the posters home and using them as insulation for the walls.
So far, the posters ⁷*will have been/have been* valued at $280,000 but the renovation work still isn't finished and there may be more treasures. Winkleman, an ex-boxer who ⁸*will have worked/ has been working* as a counsellor since 2001, said he was amazed ⁹*to have been coming across/to have come across* such treasure. '¹⁰*I'd never imagined/I'd never been imagining* anything like this could happen. Next Monday, ¹¹*I've been living/I'll have been living* here two weeks and ¹²*I'll have 'earned'/I'd 'earned'* $20,000 worth of antique posters per day.'

FUNCTION EXPRESSING HYPOTHETICAL PREFERENCES

10 Read about a dilemma in a film. Then write one word in each gap to complete the conversation.

> ⑫ **THE BOX** ·
>
> **Screen 1: 2p.m., 6p.m., 8.30p.m.**
>
> A character is presented with a dilemma: if she pushes a button, she will receive a payment of $1,000,000 but somewhere in the world someone who she doesn't know will die.

Rod: It's an interesting idea, but ¹_____ way would I sacrifice a human life just for money. Without a shadow of a ²_____, I'd refuse to push the button.

Ulrich: I sort of agree, but there might be exceptional circumstances. For example, if the million dollars could pay for an operation to save a child's life and it was, say, a very sick hundred-year-old who was going to die … Obviously, ³_____ the choice, I'd rather not be the person pushing the button, but …

Rod: No, whatever the circumstances, far better ⁴_____ let fate decide.

Ulrich: Well yes, my preference ⁵_____ be to leave it to fate, but if I ever found ⁶_____ in this situation, I'd have to think hard about it.

Rod: So what would you have done if it was you in the film?

Ulrich: If it was ⁷_____ to me, I'd have asked for more information about the circumstances of the person's death!

Rod: I don't think that was part of the deal!

Ulrich: I know. What about you?

Rod: I'd just say a straight 'no' and walk away. That would be ⁸_____ far the best option.

CHECK

Circle the correct option to complete the sentences.

1 Dad likes noisy towns, but I prefer _____ places where you can relax in peace.
   a) bustling   **b)** ancient   **c)** tranquil

2 We shouted, but no one replied. The place was completely _____.
   a) unspoilt   **b)** deserted   **c)** picturesque

3 We lived in a _____ village.
   a) little busy fishing   **b)** fishing busy little
   c) busy little fishing

4 Mel brought a _____ cake to my party.
   a) homemade chocolate delicious
   b) delicious chocolate homemade
   c) delicious homemade chocolate

5 She arrived with her _____ John, who we'd heard so much about.
   a) handsome ex-policeman boyfriend
   b) handsome boyfriend ex-policeman
   c) ex-policeman handsome boyfriend

6 My first apartment was a _____ little place with bad lighting and no space.
   a) gaudy   **b)** roomy   **c)** poky

7 This courtyard is nice and _____. It'll keep us out of the sun for a while.
   a) dreary   **b)** shady   **c)** ancient

8 I read the list of prize winners, some _____ names seemed familiar.
   a) of whom   **b)** of which   **c)** of whose

9 That's the song _____ my brother played bass guitar.
   a) that   **b)** on whom   **c)** on which

10 They called my name at 4.00, _____ I'd fallen asleep.
   a) by which time   **b)** at that time   **c)** by that time

11 They beat us by playing well and because we'd _____ them.
   a) overestimated   **b)** underestimated
   c) estimated

12 It was all a terrible _____.
   a) misunderstanding   **b)** non-understanding
   c) mal-understanding

13 I'll start by _____ a bit of background information about the idea.
   a) telling   **b)** giving   **c)** making

14 The _____ benefit is that, in fifty years, our company will still be here.
   a) highest   **b)** short-term   **c)** long-term

15 We managed to _____ a solution to the pollution problem.
   a) come up to   **b)** think up with   **c)** come up with

16 The accused man _____ his innocence, but he was convicted.
   a) protested   **b)** said   **c)** fought

17 She made _____ against her sentence, so there was another trial.
   a) a complaint   **b)** a protest   **c)** an appeal

18 I try not to scratch the itch, but I _____!
   a) have it done   **b)** made it   **c)** can't help it

19 If you could help us, we'd _____.
   a) appreciate it   **b)** appreciate
   c) appreciate for it

20 _____ that a cleaner has won a lottery worth $45,000,000.
   a) It seems reported   **b)** It's been reported
   c) There's been reported

21 We need to bring criminals like him _____ immediately.
   a) for justice   **b)** to justice   **c)** justice

22 Thousands hit the streets _____ justice for the accused.
   a) appealing   **b)** protesting   **c)** demanding

23 You look exhausted. _____ all night?
   a) Had you been working   **b)** Have you worked
   c) Have you been working

24 I'm fed up! By 5.00 I'll _____ in this office for six hours!
   a) wait   **b)** have been waiting   **c)** have waited

25 The missing person seems _____ contacted anyone for several days.
   a) to not have   **b)** that he hasn't   **c)** not to have

26 Will this law affect our _____ liberties?
   a) civil   **b)** civilian   **c)** human

27 _____ between our countries will benefit everybody.
   a) Trade free   **b)** Free economics   **c)** Free trade

28 Without a shadow of _____, this is the best thing to do.
   a) the doubt   **b)** a doubt   **c)** thought

29 If it was up _____ me, I'd go to Hamburg.
   a) to   **b)** for   **c)** by

30 That idea is _____ of the question. It's too expensive.
   a) not   **b)** off   **c)** out

RESULT   **/30**

5)) SECRETS

VOCABULARY

IDIOMS: SECRETS

1 A Complete the conversations.

1 **A:** Come on! Tell us what happened when you arrived.
  B: Yes, go on. Spill the _____ .

2 **A:** Oh dear. That was close. I nearly gave the game _____ .
  B: Really? What did you say?

3 **A:** I think I might have let it _____ that we're planning a party.
  B: Davide! That's supposed to be a secret.

4 **A:** Can I tell you something about the management committee?
  B: Sure. I promise I'll _____ schtum if anyone asks me.

5 **A:** They are so secretive.
  B: I know. I'd love to know what goes on behind closed _____ .

6 **A:** I can't believe I told him you were planning to leave. I'm sorry.
  B: Yes, you really let the _____ out of the bag.

B ▶ 5.1 Listen and check.

GRAMMAR

MODAL VERBS AND RELATED PHRASES

2 Underline the correct alternative.

1 I'm worried about Eva. I *should/must* have told her the truth.
2 'Do you know how they got together?' 'I think they *may/should* have met when they were at college.'
3 I *had to/must* leave my job because I couldn't stand it anymore.
4 If we're going to be late, I think we *ought/'d better* call her.
5 You're *ought/supposed* to be able to open the box here.
6 You *didn't need/needn't* have brought your laptop after all. We've got one already.
7 Guido's planning on becoming a tour guide. I *couldn't/shouldn't* do that. I'd hate it.
8 You'd *better not/shouldn't* mention that you saw me here. That would give the game away.
9 Sometimes telling the truth *can/can't* get you into more trouble than it's worth.
10 We *must/ought* leave before the police get here!

3 Complete the second sentence so that it has a similar meaning to the first. Use the words in the box and any other necessary words.

> banned   compulsory   dared   forced   permissible

1 All employees must attend these boring weekly meetings.
  The boring weekly meetings _____ all employees.
2 Student protests may be disallowed if the violence continues.
  Student protests _____ the violence continues.
3 The police officer was made to retire after thirty-two years.
  The police officer _____ thirty-two years.
4 From then on, nobody had the courage to ask any more questions.
  From then on, _____ any more questions.
5 I'm afraid that this kind of behaviour is simply not allowed.
  I'm afraid that _____ .

READING

4 A Read the text opposite and circle the correct answers.

1 Where did the writer find the letters?
  a) in the corner of the kitchen
  b) in the corner of an old dresser
  c) under a door in the kitchen

2 Why were the early months in France difficult?
  a) She couldn't speak the language.
  b) She was living in the middle of nowhere.
  c) Her husband was dying.

3 What kind of letters were they?
  a) personal family correspondence
  b) official letters from the army
  c) love letters from a soldier

4 Why was the mother's letter inconsiderate?
  a) She seemed unaware of how difficult things were for her son.
  b) She tells the son private information about his wife.
  c) She seemed oblivious to how prices were changing.

5 How does the son react to his mother's letter?
  a) He writes to tell his mother he wishes to have no more contact with her.
  b) He writes to ask his mother to try and be more understanding.
  c) He writes to his wife complaining about the mother's behaviour.

6 What does the writer plan to do with the letters?
  a) She would like to return them to the family.
  b) She plans to publish them as a book.
  c) She wants to give them to her grandchildren.

B Complete the sentences with the underlined words from the text.

1 She spoke _____ about her experiences during the war.
2 The writing was so small, I could _____ see who had written the letter.
3 The extremely harsh weather was difficult to _____ .
4 We wrote to her parents _____ them for their help in the matter.

Dearest Mother,

Secrets from the past

We had been in the old French farmhouse <u>barely</u> two months when my husband received the most terrible news. He was poorly and, as it turned out, he had only a few months to live. You can imagine then that the following months, living alone in the French countryside, were difficult. When the long winter was over, I decided to clear out the house and rearrange the furniture, putting fresh paint on the walls and re-planting the garden. I wanted the house to look as my husband would have liked it.

It was when I took the heavy wooden doors off the antique dresser in the kitchen that I found a small brown package tucked up into one of the corners. It was a handful of letters, some hand-written, others typed. They had been wrapped in brown greaseproof paper. I sat at the old kitchen table and carefully unwrapped them one by one. The letters were dated 1917 and were the correspondence between a British mother and her soldier son, who had obviously been sent to France during the First World War. As I read the words sent between the two, I wept.

The first was a letter from the mother in which she seems quite oblivious to the hardships her son is having to <u>endure</u> on the front line. She complains of the price of coal and vests but, most <u>poignantly</u>, she bitterly criticises the behaviour of the young soldier's wife, now heavily pregnant. She complains that the young wife did not invite her mother-in-law to spend time with them before the soldier left for France.

I read the son's reply to his mother in which he calmly explains his love for his wife and their desire to spend some time alone now that they are married. He ends by <u>imploring</u> his mother to have more patience and be more open-minded and understanding towards his new wife. He says, 'Now is not the time for quarrelling. If you were in my position, or my brother's, you would realise more fully what it is to be miles away from your own fireside, not knowing when death may overcome you.'

It was the most extraordinary feeling to hold the letters in my hands. I felt as if I was intruding on their most private correspondence – secrets from the past – and I so desperately hoped that the young man had returned safely home to his loved ones. I have since been trying to contact the family. I'm hoping that perhaps one of the grandchildren or great grandchildren will be alive today so that I can pass on the letters which form such an intimate part of their family history.

WRITING

A NARRATIVE; LEARN TO USE TIME PHRASES

5 A Choose the correct time phrases to complete the story.

Sonia Gonzalez's parents were Mexican immigrants who had moved to the USA ¹_____ after she was born. However, ²_____ things hadn't worked out quite as they might have planned. Although her parents ³_____ meant to learn English, neither of them did, so Sonia's father often struggled to find work. Life wasn't easy and, ⁴_____, Sonia grew up quickly out of necessity. Sonia's mother always seemed to be pregnant and spent most of her time lying in bed or watching television ⁵_____ Sonia was left to clean and tidy the house and look after her younger brothers. ⁶_____, there were many rows. One day, ⁷_____ an argument when Sonia tried to finish her schoolwork before dealing with the family chores, her mother decided that it was time for her to visit her grandmother in Mexico and learn 'the ways of the old world' and the importance of 'la familia'. ⁸_____, a trip was planned and Sonia headed south to visit her cousins. ⁹_____ she met her wise grandmother, Sonia knew that here was someone who understood her. The old woman could see ¹⁰_____ that Sonia had dreams that would take her far beyond her mother's expectations.

1 a) eventually   b) immediately
  c) meanwhile
2 a) from then on   b) in the meantime
  c) as soon as
3 a) afterwards   b) while
  c) originally
4 a) in the meantime b) previously
  c) as soon as
5 a) while   b) after
  c) since
6 a) The moment   b) Subsequently
  c) Ever since
7 a) ever since   b) afterwards
  c) after
8 a) Eventually   b) In the meantime
  c) Just before
9 a) Instantly   b) Immediately
  c) As soon as
10 a) the moment   b) instantly
   c) ever since

B Write a paragraph to end the story (100–150 words). Include two or three of the time phrases from the text.

GRAMMAR
THE PASSIVE

1 Choose the correct options to complete the text.

A HOLLYWOOD TALE

For years, a romantic story [1]_____ about Hollywood wonder-boy Steven Spielberg. According to legend, the director managed to infiltrate Universal Pictures when he was a high school student.

The story goes like this: the precocious 17-year-old was on a tour of the studio when he escaped during a toilet break and [2]_____ caught by a man who worked there. Spielberg expected [3]_____ to leave, but the man [4]_____ out. Instead, he chatted to Spielberg and gave him a pass to get into the studio the following day, which Spielberg used.

The day after that, Spielberg had no pass but, determined to enter the studio again, he put on a black suit, took his father's briefcase and bluffed his way past the guard. The briefcase contained nothing but a sandwich and two candy bars.

[5]_____ said that Spielberg played the same trick every day for the rest of the summer, wandering around film sets, rubbing shoulders with actors, directors and writers. One day, the story goes, he came across a room that [6]_____. He set up an office, put his name on the door, went to the main switchboard, introduced himself and [7]_____ him an extension number so he could receive calls. [8]_____ claimed that it was two years before he was discovered by the bosses at Universal Pictures.

The story, it turns out, is a wild exaggeration. The teenaged Spielberg [9]_____ given a phone extension for two years. In truth, he didn't even have an office. He was introduced to Hollywood by a friend of his father and, rather than wandering around freely, Spielberg [10]_____ employed doing paperwork.

So Spielberg's introduction to the business [11]_____ as a myth. But is that surprising or [12]_____ expected? This, after all, is Hollywood, the land of myths and heroes.

1 **a)** is being told **b)** is telling **c)** has been told
2 **a)** was **b)** had been **c)** must be
3 **a)** to ask **b)** that he ask **c)** to be asked
4 **a)** didn't have him throw
  b) didn't have him thrown **c)** had him not thrown
5 **a)** That's **b)** It's **c)** It
6 **a)** wasn't being used **b)** wasn't been used
  c) didn't use
7 **a)** had assigned **b)** had the operator to assign
  c) had the operator assign
8 **a)** It's also **b)** It has also **c)** What's also
9 **a)** hadn't **b)** wasn't to be **c)** wasn't
10 **a)** was **b)** was to have **c)** had
11 **a)** is to recognise **b)** is now recognised
  c) is recognising
12 **a)** it is to be **b)** is it to be **c)** is it for being

2 Complete the sentences with suitable words. All the sentences contain passives or causatives.

1 What can _____ _____ about the problem of global warming? 'A lot,' say scientists.
2 Today there _____ thought _____ _____ around 400 types of cheese in France.
3 When she was ten, Gracie _____ her wisdom teeth _____ out.
4 It _____ said that ghosts have _____ seen in this castle.
5 All bills must _____ _____ by the first of the month.
6 Oh no! My car _____ _____ stolen! I can't see it anywhere.
7 Dom's never this late. He must _____ _____ _____ the wrong directions by Nick.
8 That medicine is _____ to _____ _____ more than twice a day. It's very strong.
9 Hooray! This Christmas, everyone in the office _____ _____ _____ a €1000 bonus.
10 1940s legend Joe Louis is often said _____ _____ _____ the greatest boxer in history.
11 My mother _____ _____ _____ on by the surgeon right now. It's a simple procedure.
12 He _____ his son _____ to us for the mess, so the kid came over and said 'sorry'.

VOCABULARY
TRUTH OR MYTH

3 Complete the second sentence so that it has a similar meaning to the first. Use three words, including the word given.

1 Can you prove that this is true?
  VERIFY
  Are you able _____?
2 In the 1950s, people believed that smoking did no harm.
  CONVENTIONAL
  In the 1950s, _____
  was that smoking was harmless.
3 We need to expose that myth.
  DEBUNKING
  That _____.
4 No one believes that myth anymore.
  DISPROVED
  That myth _____.
5 The journalist decided to reveal the facts.
  UNCOVER
  The journalist decided to _____.
6 Many people think bats are blind.
  HELD
  The idea that bats are blind is a
  _____.

LISTENING

4 A Read the definition of an urban myth. What urban myth do you think is shown in the picture?

> **urban myth** *n*: a shocking or sensational story that spreads via different media. Many people believe it is true despite little or no evidence.

B ▶ 5.2 Listen to a radio interview to check your answer.

C Listen again and circle the correct answers.

1 Who believes the myth, according to the presenter?
   a) no one
   b) almost everyone
   c) plenty of intelligent people

2 What metaphor does the guest speaker mention?
   a) alligators as danger and darkness
   b) the city as an urban jungle
   c) cities as monsters

3 How did the urban myth start?
   a) Baby alligators were found in sewers in Florida.
   b) Teenagers put an alligator in the sewers in the 1930s.
   c) New Yorkers were said to flush their pet alligators down the toilet.

4 Who was Robert Daley?
   a) a man who wrote a book about New York's utilities
   b) the superintendent of city sewers
   c) a teenager who found an alligator in the sewers

5 Why did Teddy May go into the sewers to investigate?
   a) because he was doing some research for a book
   b) because he wanted to see alligators
   c) because his workers said they'd seen alligators

6 What does the speaker say about Teddy May?
   a) He was quite famous for telling unbelievable stories.
   b) He was a reliable witness because he had worked in the sewers for a long time.
   c) He carried a gun to work in case he saw alligators.

7 Why do scientists think it's unlikely that alligators live in the sewers?
   a) Alligators need a more varied diet than they can get in the sewers.
   b) Alligators wouldn't survive the cold, pollution and darkness.
   c) Alligators cannot live in the presence of so many rats and cockroaches.

VOCABULARY PLUS

MULTI-WORD VERBS

5 The pairs of sentences are missing the same preposition. Decide which preposition is missing and add it to both sentences in the correct place.

1 a) John and the gang are hanging ⟨*out*⟩ in the car park.
   b) I only just found ⟨*out*⟩ about your great news. Congratulations!

2 a) She was hurt quite badly, but she soldiered till the end.
   b) Don't wait for me – I'm going to be late. You just carry.

3 a) The government is planning to crack on antisocial behaviour.
   b) You'd better slow – that pedestrian hasn't seen you.

4 a) She spent hours poring those documents and found nothing.
   b) If you have a problem, you can talk it with me.

5 a) Don't just stand watching us work – help us!
   b) You can't mess here in the factory – it's too dangerous.

6 a) I'm just going to put these dishes.
   b) That concert was amazing. We were completely blown.

7 a) You're working too slowly. You need to speed.
   b) He added some avocado and feta cheese to jazz the salad.

8 a) I think they'll pension me next year. I'll be seventy by then.
   b) The match was called because they couldn't raise a team.

9 a) Seeing you again brings lots of memories of school.
   b) Try to think to your childhood; what can you remember?

10 a) James really stands in the crowd wearing that enormous hat!
   b) You know I'm always prepared to speak against injustice, wherever I find it.

VOCABULARY
JOURNALISM

1 Complete the crossword.

(crossword grid with numbers 1, 2, 3, 4, 5, 6)

Across

3 Do I need to take out an _____ to stop the story being published?

4 I've heard from a reliable _____ that the company is in trouble.

5 Ajay lost his job when it was discovered he was the source of the _____.

6 It was thought that the man had access to _____ information regarding national security.

Down

1 Documents on Wikileaks are _____ anonymously.

2 His main interest lay in _____ journalism, where he could work like a detective to uncover the story.

6 The newspaper had a major _____ by getting the story ahead of their rivals.

FUNCTION
MAKING A POINT

2 Write sentences with the prompts and your own words.

1 what / basically / saying / depends / final result

_____

2 point / I / trying / make / that / we / can't afford / waste time

_____

3 facts / suggest / that / high prices / are / consequence / shortage in demand

_____

4 do / think / that / always / case?

_____

5 is / any / way / prove / that?

_____

6 if / you / think / about / it / simply / doesn't / make / sense

_____

7 can / we / sure / this?

_____

8 let / put / this way / the company / going / out of business

_____

LEARN TO
MANAGE A CONVERSATION

3 A Complete the conversation with the words in the box.

> another   don't   feel   going   hold   interesting
> stand   suppose   think   wanted

A: So, what do you [1]_____ about the issue of downloading music from the internet? How do you [2]_____ about it?

B: Well, it's an [3]_____ question to consider. I [4]_____ if you think about it, everyone should always pay for their music because that's how the musicians earn their money.

C: That's right. Because if you want to listen to music which …

B: [5]_____ on a minute. I [6]_____ to say that the problem is that music companies charge so much for music sometimes. That's why people are tempted to download for free.

C: But [7]_____ you think that we *should* be allowed to download for free? It helps the band to become popular and then they can make their money from doing live music gigs and things like that; or from selling T-shirts and other merchandise – coffee mugs and …

A: Yes. But [8]_____ back to what you were saying about musicians earning money from writing songs: surely they should be paid for that, too? Where do you [9]_____ on that?

B: Absolutely. I mean, they can make money in other ways, but the music is their intellectual property and they should be paid for it.

C: Sorry, and [10]_____ thing. If a band is popular, so people have downloaded lots of their music, then they'll be invited to festivals. There are lots of other ways they can still make money.

B: Yes, but the point I'm trying to make is that they shouldn't have to give their music away for free.

C: It's not something I've thought about before, but …

B ▶ 5.3 Listen and check.

C Look at the conversation again and underline the expressions used to manage the conversation.

D ▶ 5.4 Listen and check. Then listen again and repeat.

VOCABULARY

PREDICTIONS

1 Circle the correct options to complete the text.

Three predictions about travel in the next fifty years

The [1]_____ are that the rising cost of oil will make air travel all but obsolete except for the super-rich. Current figures [2]_____ to the fact that prices may reach €10,000 for just a short trip abroad, and the days of zooming across Europe for the price of a coach ticket will be nothing but a [3]_____ memory. 'Staycations' and virtual tours of exotic places will replace vacations, making a serious dent in the tourist industry.

The [4]_____ that cars will downsize. Those gas-guzzling monsters that fill the roads today will soon become a [5]_____ of the past. Law-makers are [6]_____ to intervene in favour of eco-friendly cars, while people will believe 'smaller is better' as the number of parking spaces fails to grow in proportion to the population. The development of intelligent cars means that, by 2030, they will drive themselves.

Train travel [7]_____ a big boom area. Following the growth in usable bio-fuels, small, compact trains will be everywhere, regularly filling up at bio-fuel stations. The train is also [8]_____ to be silent. Acoustic technicians may [9]_____ have come up with sound-neutralising frequency waves that mute the carriage. The [10]_____ of being deafened by engines and mobile phone conversations will be over.

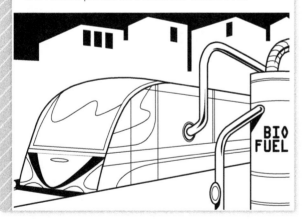

1 a) opportunities   b) truths   c) signs
2 a) point   b) signal   c) target
3 a) long   b) far   c) distant
4 a) facts suggest   b) figures point to
   c) may well
5 a) moment   b) thing   c) memorial
6 a) for   b) bound   c) definite
7 a) is destined to be   b) the signs are
   c) is no longer
8 a) ready   b) likely   c) thought
9 a) right   b) well   c) but
10 a) days   b) day   c) time

GRAMMAR

FUTURE FORMS

2 Cross out the option which is not possible.
1 The government _____ introduce a new tax on imports next year.
   a) is due to   b) could be to   c) is to
2 We can't visit them now because it's midnight and they'll _____ bed.
   a) be in   b) have been in   c) have gone to
3 We will _____ there because it's a lot quicker than driving.
   a) fly   b) be flying   c) be to fly
4 By the time you next see me, I'll _____ here for six months.
   a) have been living   b) have lived   c) live
5 I think my team _____ the cup this year.
   a) is going to win   b) is winning   c) will win
6 This time next week I _____ on a beach in Thailand!
   a) 'm going to be lying   b) am due to lying
   c) 'll be lying

3 Underline the correct alternatives.

How will your profession have changed by 2030?

Cooking with organic products will [1]*have become/be being* the norm by 2030. I also think we'll [2]*have used/be using* more vegetable products as society changes its attitude towards animals.   (PETRUS WIESE, CHEF)

I've heard that in some countries, schools are [3]*for introducing/to introduce* interactive smart boards in every classroom. This might have an impact but teaching [4]*looks to/will* be largely the same as it is now in most subjects.
(IRINA KASINSKYEV, SCIENCE TEACHER)

In 2030 India [5]*is/will* due to overtake China as the world's most populous country. This will be a massively important moment because India [6]*is going/could* to become a major political power on the back of its numbers.
(CALLUM MCBRIDE, HUMAN GEOGRAPHER)

My profession [7]*couldn't/won't* exist. We will have [8]*been destroying/destroyed* the fish population and ruined the industry by over-fishing.
(STEPHEN KNOX, FISHERMAN)

By 2030, we'll [9]*have developed/be to develop* self-growing organs that can be used by accident victims or patients with genetic diseases. In fact, this [10]*could be/will have been becoming* a reality as early as 2020.
(MARGARITA ORTAL, MEDICAL BIOPHYSICIST)

By 2030, we will [11]*be/have been* reading books in some form for over 4,000 years, so I think their complete demise is unlikely. They may get less popular, but they [12]*aren't going to disappear/won't have disappeared* any time soon.   (ROGER LEVINE, PUBLISHER)

4 A Complete B's answers using the prompts. Use future forms and contractions.

1 **A:** What will your life be like in 2020?
  B: I _____ famous. (become)

2 **A:** How will your work have changed by 2020?
  B: It _____ much. (not / change)

3 **A:** What anniversary are you celebrating tomorrow?
  B: We _____ for ten years. (marry)

4 **A:** What time does the match start?
  B: We _____ there at 1.00. (need / be)

B ▶ 6.1 Listen and check. Pay attention to the use of contractions.

C Listen again and repeat B's answers, making sure you use contractions in the correct places.

LISTENING

5 A ▶ 6.2 Listen to part of a lecture about ways of foretelling the future. Number the pictures in the order they are discussed.

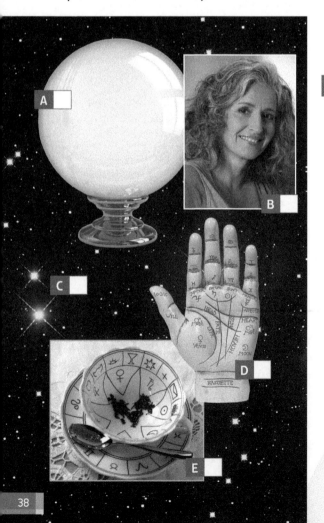

A
B
C
D
E

B Listen again and complete the sentences with one or two words.

1 A canary will choose a _____ that reveals your fortune.

2 Telling the future by examining the intestines of dead animals began in Babylon and was continued by the _____ and Romans.

3 To read the future, we have looked at _____ and at the skies.

4 The science that tells the future by looking at the stars is called _____.

5 The technique of examining the face to tell the future began in _____.

6 Physiognomists take _____ _____ to be trained.

7 Palm readers believe that aspects of our lives correspond to the _____ on our hands.

8 The most famous object associated with fortune telling is the _____ _____.

C Circle a word in each extract 1–6 which matches one of the definitions a)–f). Write the correct letter.

1 a Nepalese (shaman) examines the intestines …   c
2 Julius Caesar himself used a seer to predict his own future.
3 … man has always sought to read his future,
4 what will happen to me and my kin?
5 Clues to emotional and physical health are found in the face, as well as personality traits,
6 … remnants of past events and signals of events yet to come.

a) particular qualities in someone's character
b) small parts of something that remain after the rest has gone
c) tribal religious leader who talks to spirits and cures illnesses
d) looked very hard to find something
e) someone who can see into the future and say what will happen
f) family

VOCABULARY PLUS

PREPOSITIONAL PHRASES

6 Complete the text with the correct prepositions.

NOSTRADAMUS
the prophet for all the ages

Michel de Nostredame (1503–1566) is [1] _____ far the world's most famous futurologist. His predictions have been pored over, debated and interpreted for centuries. Were the 946 'quatrains' that he wrote really the work of an extraordinary prophet who'd predicted everything from the discovery of electricity to the 2001 attack on the World Trade Centre? Or is his work, [2] _____ effect, useless?

Much of Nostradamus' life remains [3] _____ of sight. We are told he was a skilful physician who treated patients during the Black Death; other accounts say he found himself [4] _____ danger during the Inquisition and, [5] _____ risk of being tried for heresy (thousands were put [6] _____ trial for their beliefs), he fled his land. He may have served as an advisor to the King of France and was, allegedly, influential in [7] _____ least three other royal households.

Knowing so little about him, after five hundred years we would expect his work and reputation to be [8] _____ decline. But it isn't. [9] _____ present, there are dozens of films about him, numerous Nostradamus societies and countless cafés, restaurants and games that bear his name. It all begs the question: did he himself know that his fame would stretch so far into the future?

VOCABULARY
LANGUAGE

1 A Complete the crossword.

Across

3 Most organisations have rules about not using _____ or strong language in the workplace.

5 Where language difficulties cause communication problems, we can say there is a language _____.

6 Your ability to use appropriate language in a variety of situations is your _____ of a language.

8 A language which is no longer spoken is a _____ language.

Down

1 A language which is spoken all over the world is a _____ language.

2 The _____ language of Brazil is Portuguese.

4 We can call the informal language people use on the streets _____ language.

7 You should _____ your language and refrain from saying things which might offend people.

B Find and correct the mistake in each of the sentences below.

1 Her mind of French is fantastic. She can deal with any kind of situation.

2 I wouldn't be at all surprised if Mandarin or Farsi soon become barrier languages, spoken all around the world.

3 I simply don't understand the point of studying an offensive language, like Latin.

4 When my parents are around we have to command our language!

5 South Africa has eleven global languages, but many other languages are commonly spoken, too.

6 It's a really difficult working situation because of the language mind between those who don't speak Spanish and those who do.

7 The broadcasters received complaints about the everyday language used in the news interview.

8 My official Greek is OK for getting around and buying things in shops and cafés, but I can't discuss politics or anything like that.

GRAMMAR
CONCESSION CLAUSES

2 Match 1–6 with a)–f) to make sentences.

1 Even though there are many advantages to working a night shift,

2 He took us to the most wonderful restaurant,

3 Whilst I take your point,

4 Although we had only known each other for a short time,

5 Strange as it seemed to the rest of the family,

6 Despite the dreadful weather,

a) my brother and I rarely spoke.

b) despite not really being able to afford it.

c) we had a fantastic holiday.

d) most people consider that the disadvantages outweigh any financial gain.

e) I'm afraid I can't agree with what you're saying.

f) we felt like best friends.

3 Find and correct the mistake in six of the sentences.

1 Strange as it may seems, we were the only people left at the end of the party.

2 Despite have such a huge influence, he was unable to secure the deal.

3 Whichever way you looking at it, it's still a really good deal.

4 In spite the surge in oil prices, ministers have assured us that petrol prices will remain stable.

5 Whilst they chatted and laughed, we were busy organising everything.

6 However we going about things, it's not going to be an easy assignment.

7 Even if had we managed to identify the criminal previously, we would never have been able to trace the jewels.

8 Although the slope seemed easy to climb at first, it became gradually more difficult the higher we went.

READING

4 A Look at the statements and decide if they are true (T) or false (F).

1 You can use the exclamation 'D'oh' when you have done something foolish.

2 Marketing companies and politicians are reducing the number of catchphrases they use.

3 Shakespeare's writing encouraged the adoption of new words and phrases into the English language.

4 If someone is too relaxed and laid-back in their attitude to work, you can say they need to 'take a chill pill'.

5 President Obama used the catchphrase 'Make no mistake' nearly 3,000 times in his first two years of office.

6 The use of catchphrases is a trend which will soon die out.

B Read the article below to check your answers.

WRITING

A REPORT; LEARN TO DESCRIBE TRENDS

5 A Rewrite the sentences using the correct form of the prompts in brackets and your own words.

1 There has been a dramatic increase in the number of children outside English-speaking countries who are learning English in primary school. (rocket)

2 The size of English-speaking communities in both China and India has increased sharply. (a surge)

3 There will be enormous growth in the influence of the internet on the English language. (due / increase / dramatically)

4 There is currently a rapid increase in the amount of information on the internet as it doubles its content every ten hours. (soar)

5 Until now, most internet content has been in text form but over the next ten years, there will be a sharp rise in Voice-over-Internet Protocol (VoIP). (become / dominant)

6 The amount of written text on the internet will gradually decrease. (a steady decline)

B Use your sentences to write a report on the factors influencing the English language (250–280 words).

'D'oh!'
is our favourite catchphrase

Homer Simpson's catchphrase 'D'oh!' has been voted the greatest contribution made by the famous yellow cartoon family to the English language, beating other much-loved catchphrases from the long-running sitcom, including 'eat my shorts' and 'don't have a cow'.

The exclamation 'D'oh', which can be used to express frustration that things haven't turned out quite as you might have liked them to or that you have just said or done something foolish, was officially added to the Oxford English Dictionary in 2001.

Interestingly, the last decade has seen an increase in the adoption of catchphrases, now used ubiquitously in advertising and internet marketing. In fact, characters like Homer Simpson and an increase in communications systems facilitated by the internet, have led to a 'golden age' for the invention and inclusion of new words in the English language. Not since Shakespeare's time have we seen so many new words and phrases so commonly adopted.

Consider these. Do you know someone who needs to 'take a chill pill' (a notional pill taken to calm down)? Wondering how you can afford to pay for your next holiday? Why not try a 'staycation' (a holiday spent in one's own country) instead? Can you think of anyone you'd like to 'unfriend' (or 'defriend' – remove someone from a list of friends or contacts on a social networking site)? Or have you got any 'frenemies' (people you are friendly to despite a fundamental dislike or rivalry)?

And it's not just cartoon characters who enjoy catchphrases. President Obama is pretty fond of his catchphrases, too. 'Make no mistake' is a phrase he used no less than 2,900 times during his first two years of office. Other signature Obama sayings include 'Here's the deal' (1,450 times) and 'Let me be clear,' (1,066 times). And in recognition of the tough financial times he was facing, his fifth most popular motto was 'It will not be easy.'

Experts say that by looking at the nature of the catchphrases we adopt, we get an idea about some of the underlying things going on in society at any particular point. And we can predict how powerful a catchphrase will be by how strongly it evokes an emotion. The longest-lasting catchphrases conjure up strong feelings and are memorable. There's a good reason why people will remember and use them. One thing certainly seems to be true: the catchphrase is here to stay.

VOCABULARY

TRENDS

1 Match 1–8 with a)–h) to make sentences.

1 That style of footwear became
2 That DVD spread by
3 Sometimes strange ideas capture
4 I think that trend lost
5 Sales of the toy have
6 I don't know why that style never took
7 Her books somehow struck
8 This type of phone is just a passing

a) word of mouth.
b) a chord with the public.
c) risen since the film came out.
d) the latest thing in UK clubs.
e) its appeal a while ago.
f) trend with teenagers.
g) off in Italy.
h) the imagination.

FUNCTION

DESCRIBING CAUSE AND EFFECT

2 A ▶ 6.3 Where do you think fashion designers get their ideas? Listen to Katrina, a fashion designer, talking about what inspires her. Complete the table with the information she gives.

Places	*fashion shows,*
People	
Times	

B Complete the statements about Katrina's views with the words in the box.

attributed   lead   originate   origins
result   stem   this   traced

1 A lot of trends in fashion _____ from the street.
2 Some fashion designs can be _____ to celebrities' 'looks'.
3 A-list celebrities have an image to protect. Because of _____, they take few risks with clothes.
4 Some fashions have their _____ in images from films.
5 Watching other industries, e.g. architecture, can _____ in ideas for fashion designers.
6 Some ideas for designs _____ from images in photography books.
7 Travelling can _____ to inspiration for fashion designers.
8 Full-length body suits and oversized jackets can be _____ back to the 1980s.

3 Underline the correct alternative.

1 A poor diet can bring *about/around* various health problems.
2 The game *takes/has* its origins in ancient Egypt.
3 Such thinking has led *for/to* some of the worst excesses of our age.
4 The idea is often attributed *to/on* the philosopher Nietzsche.
5 My experiences in France gave *a rise/rise* to a love of the country.
6 The company's success can be traced *back to/back* its founder.
7 Some say the technology revolution originated *in/on* Silicon Valley.
8 Those issues *grow/have* their roots in childhood.
9 The improvements stem *to/from* that brainstorming session in May.
10 Her research resulted *in/on* a great medical breakthrough.

LEARN TO

SUMMARISE YOUR VIEWS

4 Read the summary of the recording in Exercise 2. Some lines have an extra word. Tick the correct lines and write the extra words.

To sum them up, the fashion designer describes all the	1 _____
places where she gets her ideas. What she is really	2 _____
saying about is that there are many sources for her designs.	3 _____
Basically why, fashion designers look at all kinds of images	4 _____
including film, photography books and magazines. They	5 _____
also comb the streets and small fashion shows. All in the	6 _____
all, she gives the impression that fashion designers get	7 _____
ideas from normal people on the street. Big stars don't	8 _____
take fashion risks, so to overall, designers are more likely	9 _____
to be inspired by people who aren't famous. She also says	10 _____
they look everywhere, not just in Western culture. In the	11 _____
conclusion, they are extremely inclusive about their ideas.	12 _____

GRAMMAR MODAL VERBS AND RELATED PHRASES

1 Complete the second sentence so that it has a similar meaning to the first. Use the word given.

1 She felt that she had to resign because of the scandal.
COMPELLED
She felt _____ because of the scandal.

2 He was suspended for using a substance which was not allowed.
BANNED
He was suspended for using _____.

3 You have to have car insurance.
COMPULSORY
Car insurance _____.

4 Few journalists had enough courage to cover the story.
DARED
Few journalists _____ the story.

5 As a punishment, he was not allowed to leave the house.
FORBIDDEN
As a punishment, he was _____ the house.

6 The hotel wants us to check out by 10.30.
SUPPOSED
We're _____ of the hotel by 10.30.

7 We didn't need to order so much food.
NEEDN'T
We _____ so much food.

8 They had to land the plane in a field.
FORCED
The plane _____ in a field.

GRAMMAR THE PASSIVE

2 Read the text. Some lines have an extra word. Tick the correct lines and write the extra words.

THE 10% MYTH

It is often be claimed that most people only use about 10% of their brain power.
In fact, even neuroscience students, who were asked to specify how much of
the brain is used in normal everyday activities, were answered 'about 10%'. However,
unfortunately, this is be a myth. There is no evidence to suggest that we only use
a small part of our brain. In fact, there is now plenty of scientific evidence for to
show that most of the time, when we're thinking, we are using almost all of our brain.
So, how was the myth are perpetuated? Firstly, the idea appeals to people. It's a nice
idea to think that our full potential is not being achieved, and therefore there is
room for self-improvement. The idea has been for used prolifically by marketing
people, who draw on it to help sell their products. Self-help books, for example,
which promise to help you achieve your full potential. No one knows how the myth
started, though it may have been originated from a scientific paper written by
American psychologist William James in the late nineteenth century. In the paper,
James was stated that he doubted that the average human achieved more than 10%
of their intellectual potential. Even Albert Einstein is said for to have spoken of the
10% myth with reference to his own brilliant mind; however, careful research into
the Einstein archives has been revealed no evidence of him ever making the claim.

1 ___be___
2 ✓
3 _____
4 _____
5 _____
6 _____
7 _____
8 _____
9 _____
10 _____
11 _____
12 _____
13 _____
14 _____
15 _____
16 _____
17 _____

VOCABULARY REVIEW I

3 Complete the sentences with the words in the box.

beans	cat	fallacy	game	injunction
intuitively	myth	scoop	slip	sources
verify	wisdom			

1 Lynn gave the _____ away by laughing when Kim walked in.

2 Oh no! That's let the _____ out of the bag. Now, everyone knows.

3 Come on, just spill the _____ and let us know what's happening.

4 He let it _____ that they were planning to get married.

5 She seemed to know _____ what I was talking about.

6 It's a common _____ that a neutered dog will become fat and lazy.

7 The computer program will _____ that the system is working.

8 As traffic congestion grew, the conventional _____ was to widen the roads.

9 Fellow academics later debunked the _____.

10 The newspaper generally managed to get a _____ before its rivals.

11 The judge refused to grant an _____ preventing details of the matter being published in the media.

12 A journalist should protect his or her _____.

VOCABULARY PLUS MULTI-WORD VERBS

4 Complete the adverts with the correct particles.

Do your evening meals need a little brightening ¹_____?

Don't feel you have to waste time poring ²_____ recipe books. Why not just jazz ³_____ your everyday meals with our new range of seasonings? They will surely spice up your dinner and bring ⁴_____ sweet memories of mother's home cooking.

Just take time to slow ⁵_____

Do you sometimes wonder how much longer you can carry ⁶_____ the way you are? Think ⁷_____ to the last time you felt truly relaxed. If it was more than a week ago, you need our help. Spend a day in the relaxed atmosphere of our unique health spa and give yourself time to mull ⁸_____ what is really important in your life. Don't hang ⁹_____!

Call today and book your appointment.

Do you have something you need to get off your chest?

Don't just keep ¹⁰_____ endlessly pestering your friends and family. Why not come and find ¹¹_____ more about our debating group? We meet once a week to speak ¹²_____ about concerns we have, from how the police are choosing to crack ¹³_____ on crime, to how the government plans to pension ¹⁴_____ elderly citizens. Why not come and join us? Let your voice be heard. Think it ¹⁵_____ and then give us a call on **0844 623 872**.

FUNCTION MAKING A POINT

5 Complete B's responses with the words in the box.

case evidence point put that think

1 **A:** Violent criminals deserve to die in prison.
   B: I don't see how you can say _____.

2 **A:** Bullies don't get the punishments they deserve.
   B: Do you think that's always the _____?

3 **A:** What can we do about it?
   B: The _____ is that there isn't anything we can do.

4 **A:** Can we afford to let her go?
   B: If you _____ about it, we don't have a lot of choice.

5 **A:** There is surely life on other planets.
   B: Is there any _____ to suggest that is the case?

6 **A:** How long is all this going to take?
   B: Let me _____ it this way, we don't have much time.

GRAMMAR FUTURE FORMS

6 Complete the sentences with the correct form of the verbs in brackets.

1 Don't worry. I'm sure the plane _____ _____ _____ (land) by now.

2 Have you ever wondered what you _____ _____ _____ (do) in ten years' time?

3 The government _____ (be) to pull out troops from all neighbouring countries.

4 They _____ _____ _____ (due) to arrive any minute now.

5 The new law _____ (can) spell the end of freedom of speech as we know it.

6 When you get to the station, I _____ _____ _____ (wait) for you outside.

7 There _____ _____ _____ _____ (be) a huge protest on Saturday against the suggested cuts.

8 That's fine. We _____ _____ (see) you when we get there.

VOCABULARY REVIEW 2

7 Choose the correct option to complete the sentences.

1 may well/bound
   a) The problem _____ solve itself.
   b) Mistakes are _____ to happen.

2 are over/a distant memory
   a) Her honeymoon seemed _____.
   b) I'm afraid his footballing days _____.

3 are likely/the signs are
   a) Children living in rural areas _____ to be poor.
   b) I think _____ that the economy will grow.

4 dead language/language barrier
   a) Because of the _____, it was hard for doctors to give good advice to patients.
   b) I don't see the point in studying a _____.

5 command/mind
   a) She has a wonderful _____ of the language.
   b) I had to ask him to _____ his language.

6 everyday/a global
   a) I find watching television useful for picking up bits of _____ language.
   b) The spread of Mandarin suggests that in the future it may become _____ language.

7 a chord/the imagination
   a) Her books really capture _____.
   b) Many of the things she says will strike _____ with other young women.

8 latest thing/passing trend
   a) These long, floral dresses are the _____.
   b) Interest in organic food is not a _____; it's here to stay.

9 lost its appeal/risen dramatically
   a) The number of people buying e-books has _____.
   b) I don't think cinema has ever really _____.

10 word-of-mouth/taking off
   a) The new product is already _____.
   b) The best kind of marketing for this kind of thing is _____.

GRAMMAR CONCESSION CLAUSES

8 Find and correct the mistake in six of the sentences.

1 Difficult though it seem, HTML is not difficult to learn.
2 Even if I'd warned you about the dangers, you wouldn't have listen to me.
3 However minor the problem is, I'll always ask for advice.
4 Strange as if it seems, I'm actually not very self-confident.
5 Whichever the method you choose, it will be a difficult operation.
6 In spite of know her for years, I had no idea she was involved in crime.
7 Despite be held up in traffic, we arrived on time.
8 Although it took us longer than expected, we managed to agree in the end.

VOCABULARY PLUS PREPOSITIONAL PHRASES

9 Complete the sentences with the correct preposition.

1 _____ law, seatbelts must be worn by all passengers.
2 We are _____ track to hit all our sales targets.
3 Numbers of students choosing art subjects are _____ decline.
4 We are _____ danger of having to sell the business.
5 That is _____ far the best idea we've had so far.
6 He is, _____ effect, the only person who can make the decision.
7 The children were _____ risk of abuse.
8 The poor financial results were kept _____ of sight of the investors.
9 _____ least forty people have been injured.
10 The number of drug abusers is soaring _____ of control.

FUNCTION DESCRIBING CAUSE AND EFFECT

10 Complete sentences 1–5 with phrases a)–e).

1 Mobile apps are increasingly concerned with people's emotional wellbeing. It _____ in the launch of a series of 'Happy apps' which help to improve your mood.
2 The cashless economy is slowly becoming a reality with the introduction of digital stamps and McDonald's swipe cards. The trend _____ technological advances and the consumer's desire for convenience.
3 A clothes company in Spain produces a T-shirt every month featuring consumers' photos or stories. The idea _____ the fact that stories can help to increase a consumer's emotional attachment to the product.
4 Consumers' lives continue to get busier. _____, a massive opportunity exists in selling products via subscription.
5 Consumers love to feel a sense of excitement and exclusivity. This _____ flash sales, where products are offered at a greatly reduced price without any warning and only for a very short amount of time (sometimes just for a few seconds).

a) can be attributed to
b) has resulted
c) has given rise to
d) because of this
e) originated from

CHECK

Circle the correct option to complete the sentences.

1 I don't think I should have said anything. It would have been better to _____.
   a) let it slip   **b)** stay schtum   **c)** let the cat out of the bag

2 Trust Erica to give _____ and tell everyone in the office.
   a) up the game   **b)** for the game
   c) the game away

3 Children go through eleven years of _____ education.
   a) compulsory   **b)** compulsion   **c)** compulsive

4 They reached the maximum _____ level of radiation.
   a) forbidden   **b)** permissible   **c)** allowing

5 I enjoyed the party, although I probably _____.
   a) wouldn't have gone   **b)** shouldn't go
   c) shouldn't have gone

6 Detectives worked tirelessly to _____ the truth.
   a) uncover   **b)** disprove   **c)** debunk

7 It's a commonly held _____ that Westerners don't like spicy food.
   a) truth   **b)** perception   **c)** intuition

8 Verdun _____ to be an important city in Roman times.
   a) was considered   **b)** is said   **c)** is thought

9 The drug _____ over a five-week period.
   a) has tested   **b)** is to be test   **c)** was tested

10 More research needs _____ before we can conclude that the drug is effective.
   a) to do   **b)** being done   **c)** to be done

11 I can't stand the way those youths just hang _____ on the street corner.
   a) up   **b)** around   **c)** on

12 I was completely blown _____ by their generosity.
   a) up   **b)** away   **c)** for

13 The _____ I'm trying to make is that we can't be sure.
   a) point   **b)** issue   **c)** idea

14 The evidence _____ that this is not always the case.
   a) tells   **b)** seems   **c)** shows

15 Do you think this is always the _____ ?
   a) correct   **b)** case   **c)** prove

16 The days of economic prosperity are _____.
   a) over   **b)** under   **c)** around

17 Horses as a means of transport have become a thing _____ in many places.
   a) no longer   **b)** of the past   **c)** distant memory

18 By 2050, robots like this will _____ the norm.
   a) be being   **b)** have been   **c)** have become

19 This time next year, we _____ on a beach in the Caribbean.
   a) 'll celebrating   **b)** 'll be celebrating
   c) 'll have been celebrated

20 Moon holidays _____ a reality later in the decade.
   a) could be   **b)** would be   **c)** could have been

21 What is the _____ language of Belgium?
   a) global   **b)** official   **c)** dead

22 The language _____ meant I didn't know what I was supposed to do.
   a) wall   **b)** break   **c)** barrier

23 _____ enjoying the holiday, we never went back.
   a) Despite   **b)** In spite   **c)** Even if

24 _____ way you look at it, it won't be an easy decision to make.
   a) However   **b)** Whichever   **c)** Whoever

25 _____, I would still prefer to stay in this job.
   a) Difficult though it may   **b)** Although I enjoy
   c) Strange as it seems

26 The trend for wearing massively high heels has really taken _____.
   a) up   **b)** off   **c)** on

27 Reggae music can be _____ to its roots in Jamaican folk music of the 1950s.
   a) influenced   **b)** resulted in   **c)** traced back

28 Kilo fashion, where shops sell clothes by the kilo, _____ in Milan.
   a) all started   **b)** stems   **c)** resulted

29 Your online presence is increasingly important. This has _____ companies offering their services to maintain your online reputation.
   a) given rise to   **b)** resulted   **c)** traced back to

30 This year's reduction in student numbers _____ last year's rise in fees.
   a) brought about   **b)** results in   **c)** stems from

RESULT   /30

VOCABULARY

COLLOCATIONS

1 Cross out the incorrect alternative.

1 After working an *eight-hour/early/innocent* shift, she collected her children from nursery.

2 The police *launched/lead/searched* an investigation into local corruption.

3 He suffers from *avail/asthma/amnesia*.

4 The children presumed *wrongly/extensively/rightly* that their father was dead.

5 Members of the public searched *to no avail/frantically/late* for the missing child.

6 When the lift got stuck between floors, it *launched/triggered/set off* an alarm.

GRAMMAR

CLEFT SENTENCES

2 Complete the sentences with the words in the box.

it	liked	only	place	reason	~~something~~
thing	what				

1 *Something* I have always regretted is not having spent more time with my father.

2 _____ they didn't appreciate was quite how difficult the rescue was going to be.

3 It was _____ when I chased him along the corridor that he reluctantly gave me the biscuit.

4 The main _____ why we've called you is to ask for your opinion on the matter.

5 What I _____ about the country was the openness of its people.

6 The _____ that I found most difficult to comprehend was just how lazy everybody appeared to be.

7 _____ was a miracle that the young boy was found before he came to any harm.

8 The _____ where I would most like to return to is a tiny island in the north of Greece.

3 Match 1–6 with a)–f) to make sentences.

1 It was only when we offered him money

2 The reason we failed to make the grade

3 What made me suspicious of him

4 One thing I think we should do

5 What I enjoyed most about the film

6 Something I've always wanted to do

a) is make sure we research the location more thoroughly next time.

b) was the way that he never looked you straight in the eye.

c) was the humour. It was hilarious!

d) that he decided to spill the beans.

e) is work for a charity.

f) was that we'd spent more time partying than studying.

LISTENING

4 A Look at the pictures. What do you think happened?

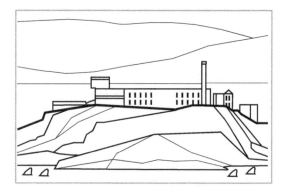

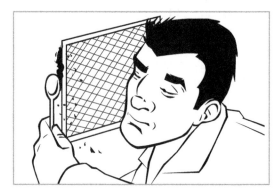

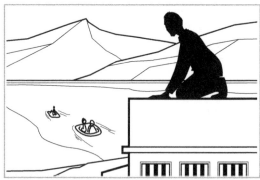

B ▶ 7.1 **Listen to the story and check your ideas.**

C **Listen again and choose the correct answers.**

1 Why were the men in prison at Alcatraz?
   a) They were convicted murderers.
   b) They were convicted bank robbers.
   c) They were convicted gang criminals.
2 How did the men plan to leave the island?
   a) They planned to steal one of the guard boats.
   b) The idea was to swim to the mainland using inflatable life vests they'd made.
   c) They planned to navigate the water using a raft and inflatable life vests.
3 How did they hope to fool the guards?
   a) by using life-like dummies which they'd made
   b) by getting other inmates to pretend to be them during head counts
   c) by using recorded voices
4 What tools did they use to dig the tunnels?
   a) a variety of stolen tools, including spoons
   b) power tools which they'd smuggled into the prison
   c) mostly spades stolen from the guards
5 Why did West not leave with the other men?
   a) He changed his mind at the last minute.
   b) He couldn't swim and was afraid of sharks.
   c) He couldn't get out of his cell in time.
6 Was the escape successful?
   a) No. All three men were later re-captured.
   b) They escaped from the prison, but it is not known whether they ever reached the shore.
   c) Yes. The men survived and made a film about it.

5 **Complete the second sentence as a cleft sentence using the prompts.**

1 The waters around the island were infested with sharks, which was a problem for the men.
   One problem for _____

2 They made a raft and inflatable life vests using stolen raincoats.
   What they used _____

3 West didn't leave with the other men because he hadn't finished digging his escape route.
   The reason _____

4 They used a system of life-like decoys to fool the guards.
   What they did to _____

5 West masterminded the whole escape plan.
   It was _____

6 The guards didn't realise that the men had already escaped.
   What _____

VOCABULARY PLUS
SUFFIXES

6 **Complete the sentences with the correct form of the words in brackets.**

1 The group remained deeply _____ (suspect) of his motives.
2 Mobile technology offers amazing _____ (opportune) to people in rural areas who have little access to education.
3 They undertook a huge _____ (renovate) project on the building.
4 His brother's unexpected _____ (reappear) was a shock to the whole family.
5 The inmates were hugely _____ (resource), using anything they could find to help dig the escape tunnel.
6 The younger generation have a _____ (tend) to lack respect for their elders.
7 We need to _____ (strong) the sides of the boat, so that we can sit on the edges.
8 With a schedule this busy, it's vital that we _____ (priority) the tasks.
9 Lack of police intervention meant the family were subjected to years of _____ (harass).
10 His originality as a composer is _____ (example) by the following pieces of music.
11 Obviously feeling the pressure, he gave _____ (evade) answers to the prosecutor's questions.
12 We hope to achieve some _____ (clear) about the situation later today.
13 The weather looks as if it might _____ (bright) up a bit later.
14 I told her I'd had a row with Pete, but she wasn't very _____ (sympathy).
15 I was just one of hundreds of _____ (apply) for the job, so I doubt if I'll get an interview.

GRAMMAR
PARTICIPLE CLAUSES

1 Tick the correct sentence in each pair.

1 a) Standing by the river, I noticed a golden fish.
  b) I noticed a golden fish standing by the river.
2 a) Being not very good with cars, I asked the mechanic to take a look.
  b) Not being very good with cars, I asked the mechanic to take a look.
3 a) I wrote the speech, helped considerably by Will.
  b) I wrote the speech, helping considerably by Will.
4 a) Having taken the medicine, I felt much better.
  b) Having been taken the medicine, I felt much better.
5 a) Exhausting from running, he lay down and slept.
  b) Exhausted from running, he lay down and slept.
6 a) Not to move a muscle, the insect watches its prey.
  b) Not moving a muscle, the insect watches its prey.
7 a) She missed the train, having failed to arrive in time.
  b) She missed the train, having failing to arrive in time.
8 a) The candidate is running for president is an old friend.
  b) The candidate running for president is an old friend.

2 Underline the correct alternatives.

[1]*Having been brought up/Bringing up* in an Italian household in the USA, Federico (Fred) Bonetti spoke little English. [2]*Having been tied/Tied* to his roots through family stories and language, and keen to get away for a short break, Bonetti decided to visit Italy. So he boarded a plane to Rome. After flying for a while, the plane made a fuel stop at JFK Airport, New York. [3]*Believing/Believed* that he had arrived in Rome, Bonetti got off the plane. [4]*Surprised/Having surprised* that his cousin wasn't there to meet him as arranged, Bonetti nevertheless took a taxi to the town centre. [5]*Not going/Not having been* to Rome before, he decided to take a look around. He couldn't help noticing that Rome's famous monuments seemed to have been replaced by skyscrapers and the street signs all seemed to be in English. [6]*Having been stopped/Stopping* to eat at a café, he also noticed that everyone was speaking in English. This, he supposed, was because so many tourists went to Rome. Tired of wandering around, Bonetti decided to make his way to his cousin's address. After wandering around in circles for several hours, he gave up and decided to take a taxi. [7]*Amazed/Amazing* that a taxi driver in Rome didn't speak Italian and [8]*not wanted/not wanting* to waste any more time, he consulted a police officer. When [9]*telling/told* he was in New York, Bonetti refused to believe it. [10]*Driving/Drove* to the airport in a police car, he insisted he was in Rome. '*This is how Italians drive!*' he said.

VOCABULARY
IDIOMS: RELAXING

3 A Underline the correct alternative.

1 Why don't you *take your time/take some time out from/give some time to* revising and go to the cinema?
2 OK, let's all have a *breath/breathing/breather*.
3 You should try to take your *mind off/mind on/brain off* the problem.
4 Don't you find it hard to *wind up/be unwind/unwind*?
5 I find it hard to *switch it off/switch off/be switched off* at the end of the day.
6 Why don't you let *some hair down/the hair down/your hair down*?

B Complete these children's jokes with sentences from Exercise 3A.

a) What did one stressed-out clock say to the other stressed-out clock?
b) What did one light bulb say to the other light bulb?

WRITING
A LEAFLET; LEARN TO USE SUBHEADINGS

4 A Read about the Freedom Festival. What is its purpose?

The **Freedom Festival** takes place next weekend. The festival includes music, dancing, local food, children's entertainment and fireworks. All money made from the festival will go to Amnesty International, an organisation that promotes freedom and justice throughout the world.

B Match subheadings 1–5 with notes a)–e).

1 Location   3 Events   5 Getting there
2 Time   4 Cost

a) €8 for adults, €5 for 12–16-year-olds, under-12s go free
b) Bus 16 or 99 from Salmouth Centre
c) 2p.m. till midnight
d) six local bands, including Firedragon; midnight firework display; bouncy castle for kids
e) Penny Park

C Read the opening lines of a leaflet to promote the event. How can you improve on it? Think about the effect on the reader. Is the message clear? Does the writer sound enthusiastic? Is it too formal/informal?

Welcome!
We would be grateful if you would attend this year's Freedom Festival. It promises to be a nice event that will help raise money for Amnesty International, a good cause. As always, we have a line-up of musicians, lots of food and fun for all the family. We are sure the event will be enjoyed.

D Complete the leaflet (200–250 words) with the subheadings in Exercise 4B and your own words.

READING

5 **A** Read the definition of a road trip. Have you ever been on one?

road trip *n* [C]: a long trip that you take in a car, usually with friends

B Read the article and answer the questions. Some questions may have multiple answers.

1 Who mentions music?
2 Who mentions the weather?
3 Who mentions people they travel with?
4 Who mentions people they meet during the trip?
5 Who doesn't mention food?
6 Who plans to sleep outside?
7 Whose road trip involves reading?
8 Whose road trips involve two wheels, not four?

C Find words/phrases in the article that match the following definitions.

1 look at something with your eyes partly closed in order to see better (introduction)

_____

2 vague; not clear or exact (introduction)

_____

3 in poor condition (Serge)

_____

4 travelled many times from one side of an area to another (Dieter) _____

5 huge amounts of empty land (Dieter)

_____

6 old, but high quality (Mike)

_____

7 with many smooth bends, e.g. a road or river (Mike)

_____

8 surrounded by views of beautiful countryside (Mike)

_____

« THE perfect road trip »

Pack up your troubles in a rucksack. Fill the tank with petrol. Squint into the distance. Step on the accelerator … and go. That was how it used to be. Now the road trip is in danger of becoming extinct in these days of super-cheap flights, rising oil prices and shrinking holiday time. But there are still those who dream of driving for weeks on end to find an unstructured, hazy kind of freedom, and even one or two who have actually done it.

I'd love to take my beaten-up old Peugeot, a box of fat novels and a cooler full of cheese and drive around Brittany for the summer. That part of France has everything – spectacular landscapes, history, wild weather and enough ghost stories to last a lifetime. Heaven!

Serge Mesnel

I've got a 1977 Harley-Davidson motorbike, heavily used. I've been all over the place – I've criss-crossed Latin America, done huge chunks of Asia and ridden the trail from Cape Town to Cairo. They were all great trips, especially Africa. The one place missing for me is Australia. I'm told the riding is good down there as it's got such vast open spaces, so that's my next trip.

Dieter Hentschel

My grand plan is to drive along the coast of Brazil stopping at little beach towns on the way. I'll take my fishing rod so I can catch my own food and my hammock so I can sleep under the stars. I think it would be an amazing adventure.

Regina Neves

It's not exactly a road trip, though we see plenty of roads. My husband and I take our bicycles to Cornwall, in the south-west of the UK, once a year and stay in a quaint little bed and breakfast. We go for excursions during the day and see all the sights like St. Ives and Land's End. I'd recommend it to anyone. When it rains we sit in a café eating scones and cream and talking to the locals. There's nothing to beat it.

Elizabeth Bell-Givens

Fifteen years ago, I went with a bunch of friends on a road trip along the west coast of the United States. We had a vintage Pontiac with a sunroof and a very loud sound system and we drove from Seattle to San Diego. We did some amazing things – hanging out in a bizarre Scandinavian town called Poulsbo, eating fresh crab in Oregon, watching street musicians in San Francisco. I remember the drive to San Diego just took our breath away. It was a long, winding highway with views of the ocean. It was just incredibly scenic and peaceful, even with Led Zeppelin on the sound system at full volume! I hope to do a similar trip along the East coast one of these days.

Mike Ashley

VOCABULARY

RISK

1 Complete the sentences with the words and phrases in the box.

> risk-averse culture   unnecessary danger
> encouraging independence   mollycoddle   deliberately
> deal with danger   unsupervised   reasonable risks

1 Children aren't allowed outside the classroom _____. They must have an adult with them at all times.

2 I don't think Toby's behaviour is helped by the fact that his over-protective parents tend to _____ him.

3 I can't believe that she would _____ expose her son to such an _____. He was standing right next to the car.

4 There's a fine line between _____, which can be seen as a good thing, and just leaving children to look after themselves, which is not such a good idea.

5 I think it's right for children to learn to take _____ so that they learn to _____.

6 People are afraid of litigation and this is what leads us to live in a _____.

FUNCTION

EXCHANGING OPINIONS

2 A Look at the picture. What would you do in this situation? Would you stop the child or let him carry on?

B ▶ 7.2 Listen to two people discussing the situation. Choose the best summary.

a) The woman thinks that the boy is being exposed to unnecessary risk and should be helped. The man argues that the boy should learn from his mistakes.

b) The man thinks that we live in a risk-averse society and children should be allowed more freedom. The woman agrees but in this case thinks that the danger is unnecessary.

3 A Correct the mistakes in the extracts. There is sometimes more than one mistake in each extract.

1 A: … if you let him carry on then you'll, then he's going to cut himself or fall into the river or something, isn't he?

　　B: Oh come off. Surely you think that?

2 A: I mean, he could fall over and hit his head on a rock or something.

　　B: Oh you're ridiculous. There's no real danger. You can't honest think that.

3 A: I suppose you've got point about thinking for yourself. It's that, as a parent, or a mother, I just think I would just naturally stop him.

4 A: I couldn't stand back and watch him hurt himself. Where's the logical in that?

5 B: Well, I'm with 100 percent you on that. But there is no accident here. It just doesn't make for sense to me. There's no real danger.

B ▶ 7.3 Listen and check.

LEARN TO

CONVINCE SOMEONE

4 A Put the words in the correct order to make sentences.

a) you / take / just / to / easy / need / I / things / think

_____

b) we / the / that / always / point / late / are / is

_____

c) think / you / idea / good / don't / a / surely / that's / ?

_____

d) joking / on, / must / come / be / you / oh

_____

e) whole / the / point / that's

_____

B Complete the conversations with the sentences in Exercise 4A.

1 A: I can't believe you gave him money. He'll just spend it on junk food.

　　B: _____ He needs to learn for himself how to spend his money.

2 A: Don't worry. We'll only be a few minutes late.

　　B: _____

3 A: I can't rest, I've got too many things to do.

　　B: That's the whole point. _____

4 A: I think we should risk it and go to the beach anyway. The forecast might be wrong.

　　B: _____ It said heavy rain and strong winds all along the coast!

5 A: We should just turn up on her doorstep and announce that we're staying for a week.

　　B: _____ Aneta would be furious.

VOCABULARY

TIME EXPRESSIONS

1 Complete the crossword.

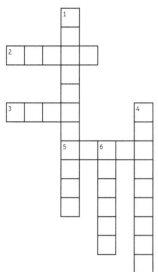

Across

2 People will remember this achievement in _____ to come.

3 Time capsules _____ back to ancient times.

5 We are _____ to enter a new era.

Down

1 People will be living under these conditions for the _____ future.

4 Items of interest are added to the collection at regular _____.

6 She was with the company from the _____; she was one of the founders.

GRAMMAR

FUTURE IN THE PAST

2 Rewrite the sentences so that they have a similar meaning. Use the prompts.

1 I forgot my ticket for the concert so I couldn't go! (supposed / go / but)

_____

2 I'd nearly left the office. The phone rang. (about / leave / when)

_____

3 You told her the secret! That wasn't the plan! (not / supposed / tell)

_____

4 We made a mistake – we didn't pay in advance. (were / meant / pay)

_____

5 I trained to be a doctor. I became a singer instead! (was / have / become / but)

_____

6 The plan was for you to be at the checkpoint at exactly 5a.m. (were)

_____

3 Choose the correct alternatives to complete the text.

The life and times of Zamp the Champ

In 1944, the U.S. War Department announced the death of former Olympic runner Lou Zamperini. His mother refused to believe it. And if he [1] _____ to be dead, Lou didn't know about it either. He was over 5,000 miles away on the other side of the world.

The son of Italian immigrants, little Lou spoke no English when his family arrived in California. Seeing that life [2] _____ be tough for him, his father taught Lou how to box. He was soon knocking out the local kids. His brother realised that thrill-seeker Lou [3] _____ to get into serious trouble so he introduced him to athletics. Zamperini started breaking records immediately and the press nicknamed him 'Zamp the Champ'

He won a scholarship to the University of Southern California and then ran in the 1936 Berlin Olympics. He later told stories about the boat trip to Europe. He [4] _____ to be in training but he gorged himself every day on the free food and put on 12 pounds. He came eighth in the 5,000 metres. Still a teenager, many thought he [5] _____ become a great runner but instead he joined the air force.

In 1943, during World War II, Zamperini's crew went out on a mission. It [6] _____ a short flight but the plane's engines failed and it crash-landed in the Pacific Ocean. Lou was trapped 70 feet underwater in a sinking plane but he managed to escape. With two other survivors, Lou spent forty-seven days on a life raft. He knew he [7] _____ die there and he kept the others going with his humour. They lived off chocolate and the birds and fish they caught with their hands.

Half-starving and exhausted, they were [8] _____ up when they saw an island. Paddling desperately, they reached the shore and were rescued by fishermen. But if they thought life [9] _____ get easier, they were in for a surprise. They spent the next two years in a prison camp.

Lou was [10] _____ to a hero's welcome but, haunted by memories of the war, he began drinking heavily. He [11] _____ the next few years in despair until he met a Christian Evangelist called Billy Graham. With Graham's help, Zamperini got his life back on track and became an inspirational speaker. In 2010, author Laura Hillenbrand ensured Lou's life [12] _____ through history when she wrote his biography, *Unbroken*.

1 a) had been **b)** supposed **c)** was supposed

2 a) is going to **b)** was on the verge of **c)** was going to

3 a) had to go **b)** was going **c)** was to have gone

4 a) meant **b)** was meant **c)** was meaning

5 a) would **b)** was on the point of **c)** was supposed

6 a) was being **b)** would be **c)** was to have been

7 a) was about **b)** wasn't meant to **c)** was on the verge of

8 a) meant to give **b)** about to give **c)** for giving

9 a) was going to **b)** was planning to **c)** was supposed

10 a) returning **b)** to return **c)** on the point to return

11 a) was spending **b)** used to spend **c)** would spend

12 a) was meant to remember **b)** would have remembered **c)** would be remembered

LISTENING

4 A Look at the pictures. What do you think the connection is between the pictures and the headline?

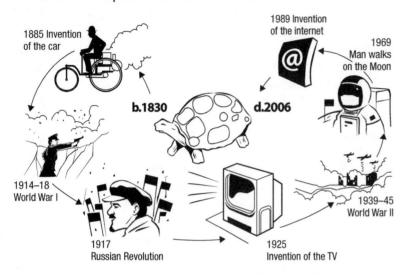

1885 Invention of the car

1989 Invention of the internet

1969 Man walks on the Moon

b.1830

d.2006

1914–18 World War I

1917 Russian Revolution

1925 Invention of the TV

1939–45 World War II

Harriet dies:

the end of a (very, very slow) stroll through time

B ▶ 8.1 Listen and check.

C Circle the correct answers. Then listen again to check.

1 What book did Harriet appear in?
a) *The Guinness Book of World Records*
b) *On the Origin of Species* by Charles Darwin
c) *Slavery in the British Empire*

2 What didn't people know about Harriet for a long time?
a) that she had a weak heart
b) that she had a connection to Charles Darwin
c) that she was a female

3 What is believed about Harriet and Charles Darwin?
a) that he looked after her the whole time she was in Britain
b) that he took her away to study her as part of his research
c) that he took her to Australia because the weather was better

4 What journeys did Harriet make?
a) from the Galapagos Islands to Britain to Australia
b) from Britain to Ecuador to Australia
c) from Australia to Britain

5 What was she like, physically, in later life?
a) she was small, about the size of dinner plate
b) she was huge
c) she had shrunk because of her age

6 How did Harriet's longevity compare with Tui Malila's?
a) Tui Malila and Harriet lived to the same age.
b) Harriet lived to an older age than Tui Malila.
c) Tui Malila lived longer than Harriet by over ten years.

VOCABULARY PLUS

PROVERBS

5 Complete the sentences with a word from A and a word from B.

A

absence	actions	built	home
judge	picture	place	practice
practise	safe	sight	ventured

B

book	day	gained	heart
heart	home	louder	mind
perfect	preach	sorry	words

1 The photo on the cover is brilliant. A _____ is worth a thousand _____.

2 The flat looks poky but it's wonderful inside. Don't _____ a _____ by its cover.

3 Once I'd left school, I forgot all my old friends. Out of _____, out of _____.

4 Do what you say you'll do, because _____ speak _____ than words.

5 I only miss him when I'm away! I guess _____ makes the _____ grow fonder.

6 I don't mind if the house takes ten years to complete. Rome wasn't _____ in a _____.

7 Why don't you try starting your own business? Nothing _____, nothing _____.

8 Work at it every day, because _____ makes _____.

9 I missed my family, my room and my stuff. I guess _____ is where the _____ is.

10 We decided not to take any risks with the car. Better _____ than _____.

11 After travelling for years, I got back and realised there's no _____ like _____.

12 You have to set a good example, and _____ what you _____.

6 A ▶ 8.2 Listen and check. Are there two or three stressed words in each proverb? Listen again and mark the stress.

B Repeat the proverbs, focusing on the rhythm.

READING

1 A Think about the following smells. What do they remind you of?

B Read the text. Were the ideas similar to your own?

THE WORLD OF SMELLS

Does the smell of freshly cut grass remind you of anything? 1_____ Inspired by the idea that smells can evoke childhood memories, I've been asking people to tell me about the smells which have this effect for them.

1 When I smell pine trees …

When we lived in Mexico, my father bought a piece of land outside Mexico City where, as kids, we used to go for picnics. I have such happy memories of that place, of everyone being together there, eating, chatting, playing around. It was in a pine forest and it was full of small, wild flowers of a thousand different colours. And the air was always fresh with the smell of pine. 2_____ The sun would peek down through the trees and touch our faces and we could feel the cool breeze. The smell of the pines would stay on our clothes for days. I'm sure that place has changed so much now. 3_____ Whenever I catch the smell of pine trees on the wind, I'm taken straight back there.

Adriana Flores Garcia

2 Baked sweet potatoes …

From when I was very young, my mother used to take me to a market in Taipei. As a treat, she would always buy me a baked sweet potato to eat from one of the market sellers. 4_____ When I held it in my hands, I didn't notice anything else. One day, I was so engrossed in eating my potato, I didn't realise where I was going and before I knew it, I was lost in the market. 5_____ In a blind panic, I ran around the stalls desperately searching. Then, not sure what to do next, I ran back to the stall where my mother had bought the sweet potatoes. The kind lady smiled at me and I stood there waiting for my mother. Eventually, she found me and stooped down to pick me up with tears in her eyes. Whenever I eat sweet potato now, I'm reminded of that day.

Sunny Kung Lee

3 After the rain …

You know that smell you get just after it's been raining? 6_____ That's the smell that reminds me of Ireland. We went travelling around Ireland a few years ago and almost everywhere we went it rained. Now, that rain smell reminds me of laughter and music in Dublin's pubs, fish and chips along the coast and the beautiful views across Galway Bay. 7_____ I can't wait to go back there again so it's a lovely reminder when it's been raining, and I can just dream of Ireland.

Cindy Brett

C Seven sentences have been removed from the article. Match sentences A–G with gaps 1–7.

A It was so hot and sweet and delicious, and I remember it was like one of the most precious things.

B I remember how my brother and I would run around there or sometimes just lie on the grass.

C It reminds me of the excited feeling of adventure I had while I was there and the kindness and hospitality we met along the way.

D The kind of damp but fresh smell; the kind of smell that makes the worms want to slither out of the ground and squirm along the pavement?

E It's probably been built on and in a way that makes the memories even more special.

F Or what about one of your favourite childhood dishes?

G My mother had vanished and all I could see were the legs of a thousand other women.

D Find words in the completed stories in the article to match definitions 1–7.

1 look quickly at something from behind something else (story 1) _____

2 valuable (story 2) _____

3 interested so much that you don't notice anything else (story 2) _____

4 bent his/her body forward and down (story 2) _____

5 slightly wet (often unpleasant) (story 3) _____

6 slide over a surface, moving from side to side (story 3) _____

7 twist from side to side or wriggle to get free (story 3) _____

GRAMMAR
ELLIPSIS AND SUBSTITUTION

2 A Write one word in each gap 1–6 to complete the conversation. Ignore the gaps in square brackets (a–m).

A: What's your earliest childhood memory?
B: I'm not sure I have ¹one. Why? What's yours?
A: Oh, I've got ²_____.
B: Have you ᵃ⁾[got lots of childhood memories]? What sorts of things can you remember?
A: Umm … ᵇ⁾[_____] my father telling me when my brother was born. I can remember that very clearly. And ᶜ⁾[_____] when I first learnt to ride my bike.
B: ᵈ⁾[_____] Bet you can't remember all the kids from school.
A: No, I can't ᵉ⁾[_____]. I can remember a few ᶠ⁾[_____] though. I guess every day was pretty much the same at school, so it's harder to remember.
B: Yeah, I suppose ³_____.
A: How about Jim Bishop? ᵍ⁾[_____] Remember him?
B: Yes, ʰ⁾[_____] course I ⁴_____.
A: ⁱ⁾[_____] Hear what happened to him?
B: No. What ʲ⁾[_____]?
A: ᵏ⁾[_____] Met a girl from Mongolia, fell in love, and moved ⁵_____ to live with her.
B: You're joking!
A: No, I'm ⁶_____ ˡ⁾[_____]. ᵐ⁾[_____] Absolutely serious.

B Look at the conversation again and add the words that were left out to the spaces in the square brackets a)–m).

3 A Cross out one extra word or add one missing word in each conversation.

1 **A:** Having a good time?
  B: Not really so.
2 **A:** See you later.
  B: Yeah … see you on there.
3 **A:** You OK with that?
  B: Yes, I think.
4 **A:** Been here before?
  B: No, never do.
5 **A:** Think they'll come back soon?
  B: I guess it's so.
6 **A:** Nearly have finished?
  B: No, I've still got lots to do.

B ▶ 8.3 Listen and check.

VOCABULARY
MEMORIES

4 Complete the sentences with the words in the box.

> ~~vividly~~ brings distinctly earliest
> flooding holds hazy vague

1 He ___vividly___ remembered the day his father left.
2 When I saw the pictures, the memories came _____ back.
3 Just the smell of that perfume _____ back memories of my grandmother.
4 This is like a trip down memory lane – this place _____ so many memories for me.
5 One of my _____ memories is of being in my pram, and leaning out to reach some strawberries.
6 My recollection of those early days when I first moved to the country is rather _____.
7 I can _____ remember the day we met.
8 I only have a very _____ memory of my grandfather. He died when I was young.

WRITING
A PERSONAL STORY; LEARN TO IMPROVE DESCRIPTIVE WRITING

5 A Complete the story with descriptive phrases a)–j).

The sweet smell of childhood

There are ¹_____ smells that I associate with my childhood but the most intense of these is my mother's perfume. She wore the same perfume for years and its ²_____ pervaded her clothes, her jewellery and much of our home.

We lived in a flat above a shop overlooking the High Street when I was growing up. The ³_____ and the pungent diesel smells from the engines of old double-decker buses would ⁴_____, choking out the fresh air. Maybe it was because of this that my mother, a lady of the sixties, a flower child, kept glass goldfish bowls filled with dried flowers and pot pourri around the house. With their delicate rose petals and ⁵_____, they would add a gentle perfume to the ⁶_____.

Having spent some time in Brazil, my mother had learnt a technique for tying headscarves tightly around her head after washing her hair, in order to dry her hair ⁷_____. The young Brazilian women had shown her how to do it. And these scarves, ⁸_____, always held onto the sweet, intoxicating smell of her perfume. I kept one when I moved to university. I suppose it was a way of taking a piece of home with me, ⁹_____ as I started on this new adventure. Smell can have an incredible effect on your mood and in moments of insecurity, I would ¹⁰_____ to my nose and breathe in the reassuring smell of home.

a) hold the silky scarf up
b) hefty fumes from the traffic
c) slightly unpleasant London air
d) a number of different
e) creep in through my open bedroom window
f) musky, exotic smell
g) as straight as a sheet
h) to comfort me
i) sweet-smelling lavender
j) with their swirly paisley patterns

B Write your own personal story (250–300 words). Use the story above as a model.

VOCABULARY

COLLOCATIONS WITH *TIME*

1 Underline the correct alternative.

1 When I'm *in a rush/pushed/crushed* for time at work, I tell my boss, 'you can have it done badly today or done well tomorrow.' It works for me!

2 When you have kids, you never have time for *itself/the self/yourself*, so I get up early in the morning and read for thirty minutes before the family wakes up.

3 I used to finish everything with time to *give/spare/relax*, but then I ended up checking it again and again. Now I finish things just before my deadlines.

4 My favourite way to *pass/use/overcome* the time when I'm bored is to hang out with an amusing friend of mine. When he's around, time always flies because I'm laughing so much.

5 I finish everything *completely/nearly/just* in time. I find that the adrenalin of a mini-panic keeps me sharp.

6 If you ever have time on your *hands/mind/day* in my profession, you should tell no one. Go and sit in a dark room, breathe deeply and enjoy it.

7 When under pressure, I go for a swim. In the water, I feel as if I have all the time in the *day/world/life*.

FUNCTION

DISCUSSING IDEAS

2 A Read the conversations about wasting time. Find and correct two mistakes in each conversation.

1 **A:** I hate being put on hold when you try to phone a company.

   B: I know how you mean.

   A: They should call you back instead of wasting your time.

   B: Yes, but looking at another way, you could end up waiting for days.

2 **A:** Ad breaks during TV programmes are the biggest waste of time.

   B: That's truly.

   A: They should have alternative versions that don't have the ads.

   B: Yeah. Minding you, that's how TV companies make their money.

3 **A:** In many companies, meetings are a complete waste of time.

   B: No and yes. It depends who's running them and what they are for.

   A: In my company, we have meetings about having meetings. Everything could be done faster and more efficiently by email.

   B: That's often the case in my company, too. Although having told that, I think it's better to discuss some things face-to-face.

4 **A:** I hate going through airport security. It's such a waste of time taking off your shoes and everything.

   B: I'm much with you there. It's a real drag.

   A: They should just give everyone a full body X-ray.

   B: That's a good idea. That makes the perfect sense.

B **8.4** Listen and check.

3 Read the statement below. Put the underlined words in the correct order to complete the responses.

> *Social networking sites are a waste of time.*
> *People should focus on real friendships.*

1 at / way / looking / another / it / but, don't you think they're a good way to meet people?

_____

2 that / said / having, those sites are fun!

_____

3 you / mind, they're great if you have friends all over the world.

_____

4 hand / the / on / other, social networking sites allow us to keep in touch with real friends.

_____

5 that / thought / I / of / never. I'm on Facebook four hours a day.

_____

6 mean / I / what / know / you. I waste loads of time on those sites.

_____

LEARN TO

SOLICIT MORE INFORMATION

4 Add or delete a word to correct the expressions in italics.

1 So, that's all for now. *Is anything we've missed?*

2 Are we finished? *Anything that to add?*

3 These are all good ideas. *What of else?*

4 Thanks, Jack. *Anyone managed to come up any other ideas?*

5 I like the basic proposition. *Can you tell to us more?*

GRAMMAR CLEFT SENTENCES

1 Read the review. Some lines have an extra word. Tick the correct lines and write the extra words.

Lush Life is about a murder in New York and the subsequent	1	✓
investigation. Though much of it the focus is on Matty, the	2	*it*
investigating officer, it's to a restaurant manager and aspiring	3	
writer called Eric who is the conscience of the novel. He	4	
witnesses the murder. What he doesn't realise is so that the	5	
police suspect him.	6	
The book is full of brilliant set-pieces. The one that sticks in	7	
the memory is the funeral procession. It's what the details that	8	
make the scene so good – the victim's half-crazy father, the	9	
band playing jazz, the 'jungle of cables and cameras'.	10	
What that I like about the book is the dialogue. It's fast,	11	
slangy and streetwise. Besides this, the thing that something	12	
strikes you is the realism. The author obviously knows the	13	
worlds of the police and the bad guys intimately. All but you	14	
can do is admire the prose and go with the relentless pace.	15	
Of something that didn't surprise me is that the author,	16	
Richard Price, writes screenplays and TV dramas such as	17	
The Wire. The dialogue and visual imagery that are stunning.	18	

VOCABULARY REVIEW I

2 Complete the second sentence so that it has a similar meaning to the first. Use the word given.

1 Who switched on the alarm?
SET
Who _____?

2 The boss is going to look into the thefts from the office.
LAUNCH
The boss is going to _____.

3 OK, everyone, relax and get your breath back.
BREATHER
OK, everyone, relax and _____.

4 I'm going to go wild at this party!
HAIR
I'm going to let _____!

5 I find it hard to stop focusing on work in the evenings.
SWITCH
I find it hard to _____.

6 I need to be distracted from all these worries.
MIND
I need to take my _____.

7 You shouldn't train so much.
TAKE TIME
You should _____.

8 You can gamble with your money, not mine!
RISKS
You can _____!

GRAMMAR PARTICIPLE CLAUSES

3 Underline the correct alternatives.
[1]*Having eaten/Eaten* dinner in Beethoven's, one of San Francisco's more expensive restaurants, US Treasury Secretary Michael Blumenthal asked to pay the bill. [2]*Telling/Told* that his Visa card had expired, he paid by cheque. The waiter, [3]*realising not/ not realising* who he was dealing with, asked for proof of Blumenthal's signature. [4]*Not having/Having* any ID on him, Blumenthal produced a dollar bill, [5]*told/telling* the waiter that, as Treasury Secretary, his signature was in the bottom corner of the bill. Suitably [6]*embarrassed/embarrassing*, the waiter accepted the cheque.

President Bill Clinton, [7]*made/having made* a quick visit to Dolly's Books in Utah, wanted to pay his bill. After [8]*handing/handed* over his American Express credit card, he waited patiently, only to be told it had expired the day before. He paid the $62.66 in cash. A similar thing happened to ex-Prime Minister of Great Britain, Margaret Thatcher. [9]*Having been attempting/Attempting* to pay for some groceries, she was surprised to be told that her cheque (unsupported by a guarantee card) had been rejected. [10]*Alerting/Alerted* to the fact that the cashier couldn't override the system for anyone, Mrs Thatcher tore up the cheque and paid in cash.

VOCABULARY PLUS SUFFIXES

4 Underline the incorrect word in each sentence and add a suffix to correct it.

1 The thing we like about text messaging is its <u>immediate</u>.   *immediacy*

2 I don't find his arguments particularly persuade.

3 A lot of those films tend to glory violence.

4 Lonely is not something that only affects the old.

5 Suffering from exhaust, she finally gave up.

6 The oldest of the siblings, he was always the dominate one.

7 Much to my embarrass, I turned up on the wrong day.

8 His reappear in London sparked all kinds of debate.

9 We need to strong our domestic policies before the election.

10 She was deep committed to social justice.

11 From an early age he'd wanted to become a music.

12 It will cost millions to modern the building.

FUNCTION   EXCHANGING OPINIONS

5 Put the underlined words in the correct order to complete the conversations.

1 **A:** I think mobile phones should be banned!
B: ¹oh / you / joking / be / come / must / on. Why?
A: Because they cause brain cancer. I read it.
B: ²that's / think / honestly / can't / you / true.

2 **A:** I think recycling should be made compulsory.
B: ³more / I / agree / couldn't.
A: And if you don't do it, you go to prison!
B: ⁴ridiculous / oh / that's!

3 **A:** I think teachers and nurses should be paid more than politicians.
B: ⁵logic / in / the / that / where's? The country would go bankrupt.
A: Because their work is just as important.
B: ⁶you've / a / suppose / point / I / got, but it wouldn't work in practice.

4 **A:** I think all business and political leaders should be women.
B: ⁷that / can / how / say / you? Some men are wonderful leaders.
A: War would almost disappear. The world would be better.
B: ⁸me / to / doesn't / just / it / sense / make.

5 **A:** I think cars should be banned from city centres.
B: Absolutely! ⁹that / you / I'm / on / with / 100 percent.
A: This will reduce pollution and traffic congestion.
B: ¹⁰right / absolutely / that's.

6 **A:** I think all workers should evaluate their bosses.
B: ¹¹up / a / I / point / to / agree / you / with.
A: And if the bosses fail their evaluation, they should be sacked.
B: ¹²practical / that's / you / surely / think / don't?

VOCABULARY   REVIEW 2

6 Add the missing letters to complete the jokes.

An old man finds that he has time on his ¹h_ _ _ _ _ so he starts meeting a childhood friend every day to talk about their ²ea_ _ _ _ st memories. 'I know we've been friends for eighty years and when I see you it ³br_ _ _ _ _ back a lot of memories, but I can't remember your name.' His friend glares at him. Five minutes pass and the friend is still glaring. Finally he says, 'How soon do you need to know?'

A couple bring their new baby home. The wife asks the husband to try changing the nappy. 'I'm a bit ⁴p_ _ _ _ _d for time. I'll do the next one,' he says. The next time the baby's nappy needs changing, she's ⁵a_ _ _ _ _ to do it when she stops and says to her husband, 'I distinctly ⁶r_ _ _ _ _ _ _r you saying you'd do it the next time'. He says, 'I didn't mean the next nappy. I meant the next baby.'

An old couple are finding that they have only ⁷h_z_ recollections of recent events so they visit a doctor. He says they should write everything down. One day they are passing the ⁸t_ _ _ _ quietly at home and she says, 'I'd love some strawberries.' 'I'll get you some,' he says. 'Some ice cream would be nice, too.' she says. 'OK,' he replies. 'And would you like some cream on top?' 'That would be wonderful,' she agrees, 'but shouldn't you write it down?' 'No! I can remember three things!' Twenty minutes pass and she's ⁹ab_ _ _t to go to the kitchen when he returns with a plate of bacon and eggs. She looks at the plate for a moment and says, 'You forgot my toast.'

GRAMMAR   FUTURE IN THE PAST

7 Write one word in each gap to complete the text.

NEVER SAY 'NO' TO E.T.

Universal Studios was about ¹_____ begin filming a crucial scene in *E.T. the Extra-Terrestrial*. Elliott, the little boy, ²_____ going to use sweets to lure E.T. into his house. The studio called Mars, Inc. about an opportunity for some product placement. They planned to use M&Ms – a brand of chocolate sweets – as E.T.'s bait, in return for which Mars, Inc. was ³_____ pay a fee or do some promotional work for the film. The studio ⁴_____ hoping to use M&Ms because of their bright colours. Rumour has it that Mars, Inc. was going ⁵_____ accept the deal but then said no. One theory for the turnaround is that a Mars, Inc. executive believed that no one ⁶_____ want to watch a film about an alien being adopted by a child. Whatever the reason, Universal Studios turned to Mars, Inc.'s rival, the Hershey Foods Corporation. Hershey's chose to use its little-known sweets Reese's Pieces. Although the company wasn't ⁷_____ to be required to pay a fee, it was meant ⁸_____ spend $1 million on advertising the film, in return for which they could use E.T. in advertising Reese's Pieces. What was to ⁹_____ been a nice little deal on a promising film turned out to be an astonishing coup. Sales of Reese's Pieces shot through the roof and *E.T. the Extra-Terrestrial* ¹⁰_____ go on to make $800 million and become one of the best-known films of all time.

VOCABULARY PLUS   PROVERBS

8 Match A, B and C to make twelve proverbs and sayings.

A	B	C
1 Actions	a) the heart	i) a thousand words.
2 A picture	b) a book	ii) than sorry.
3 Rome wasn't	c) is worth	iii) out of mind.
4 Better	d) nothing	iv) heart is.
5 Absence makes	e) built	v) preach.
6 Practice	f) safe	vi) in a day.
7 Nothing ventured,	g) sight,	vii) like home.
8 Don't judge	h) makes	viii) perfect.
9 There's no	i) place	ix) than words.
10 Out of	j) speak louder	x) by its cover.
11 Home is	k) what you	xi) gained.
12 Practise	l) where the	xii) grow fonder.

GRAMMAR   ELLIPSIS AND SUBSTITUTION

9 Circle the correct option to complete the conversations.

1 **A:** Do you think you'll get that job?
B: I expect _____.
a) yes   b) not   c) so   d) I'll

2 **A:** Remember Michael, from school?
B: Yes, I _____!
a) will   b) can   c) am   d) do

3 **A:** Lots of people at the conference this year?
B: No, not _____.
a) many   b) any   c) much   d) lot

4 **A:** Was your hard drive damaged?
B: I hope _____.
a) no   b) didn't   c) not   d) it

5 **A:** Would you like to sample this drink?
B: No thanks, but I'll try that _____.
a) ones   b) one   c) for   d) here

6 **A:** Did you go to the concert yesterday?
B: Yes, but I wish I _____.
a) didn't   b) won't   c) not   d) hadn't

7 **A:** I'm not sure the Joneses eat meat.
B: We can cook fish if they _____.
a) won't   b) haven't   c) don't   d) didn't

8 **A:** You look tired. Why don't you go to bed?
B: Once I finish this report, I _____.
a) will   b) do   c) did   d) can't

9 **A:** Can you and Heba come over for dinner?
B: We'd love _____.
a) some   b) coming   c) come   d) to

10 **A:** Don't talk to strangers when you're there.
B: Don't worry, we _____.
a) aren't   b) won't   c) shouldn't   d) don't

FUNCTION   DISCUSSING IDEAS

10 Underline the correct alternatives.

'You should try taking walks,' said Jackson.

'That's ¹*the/a* good idea. I never thought ²*of/about* that.' Peters shuffled in his chair, a faraway look in his eye.

Jackson continued. 'Having ³*told/said* that, don't walk too far. The idea is to get your brain working again, not your legs.'

'That makes perfect sense,' replied Peters. 'I'm ⁴*with/for* you there. Tell me something,' he said, leaning forward. 'Have you suffered from writer's block, too?'

Jackson eyed him like a hawk eyes its prey.

'I don't believe it exists. ⁵*Minding/Mind* you, yours is not a special case. I get people coming in here all the time whining about how they are 'blocked'. The truth is, they are only amateurs.'

'But looking ⁶*at/for* it another way, do you not think they are just lacking in inspiration?'

Jackson looked at Peters again. 'Inspiration?'

'Inspiration.'

'Do you mean like someone in your head, giving you ideas?'

'Yes and no,' said Peters. 'Um, yes, I mean ideas. Ways of finding ideas. Or on the ⁷*one/other* hand, chances to be creative, to use the imagination.'

'I know ⁸*that/what* you mean, Peters, but I'm from a different age. In my day, you simply got things done or your family didn't eat. Now go and take your walk.'

CHECK

Circle the correct option to complete the sentences.

1 _____ you don't know about can't hurt you.
   a) If   **b)** What   **c)** That

2 _____ was the butler, not the heiress, who killed him.
   a) It   **b)** There   **c)** This

3 What you do next _____ up to you.
   a) there's   **b)** that's   **c)** is

4 She _____ from frequent migraines.
   a) suffers   **b)** launches   **c)** raises

5 After a busy day at work he likes to _____ friends.
   a) unwind with   **b)** take his mind off   **c)** switch off

6 I want to take some time _____ from studying before starting university.
   a) over   **b)** down   **c)** out

7 Having _____ the song, he immediately called the band.
   a) been heard   **b)** hearing   **c)** heard

8 _____ been a pilot, he knew all about planes.
   a) After   **b)** Had   **c)** Having

9 _____ the city on horseback, they were greeted like kings.
   a) Entering   **b)** Enter   **c)** Entered

10 _____ to radiation, he knew he had little time left.
   a) Having exposed   **b)** Exposed   **c)** Exposing

11 We couldn't believe the _____ of the man.
   a) stupidly   **b)** stupid   **c)** stupidity

12 He saw a woman acting _____ so he stopped her.
   a) suspect   **b)** suspiciously   **c)** suspicious

13 I agree with you _____ to a point.
   a) up   **b)** far   **c)** through

14 None of his arguments _____ sense to me.
   a) made   **b)** took   **c)** meant

15 I suppose you've got a _____, but I'm not sure.
   a) thought   **b)** logic   **c)** point

16 We will remember their sacrifices in years to _____.
   a) go   **b)** be   **c)** come

17 I remember that holiday _____.
   a) powerfully   **b)** vividly   **c)** strongly

18 We got to Copenhagen with time to _____.
   a) save   **b)** go   **c)** spare

19 You were _____ to be here at 7.00.
   a) supposed   **b)** meaning   **c)** verging

20 You'll be working on this project for the _____ future.
   a) regular   **b)** dates   **c)** foreseeable

21 After revitalising TechGen, he _____ later become CEO.
   a) was   **b)** would   **c)** is

22 I was _____ to call you!
   a) nearly   **b)** about   **c)** almost

23 Don't judge a book by its _____.
   a) cover   **b)** promotion   **c)** author

24 Actions _____ louder than words.
   a) are   **b)** talk   **c)** speak

25 Will they leave tonight? I doubt _____.
   a) not   **b)** so   **c)** it

26 You asked if I always do my best. I try _____.
   a) it   **b)** to   **c)** so

27 Will I be fired? I hope _____.
   a) it isn't   **b)** not   **c)** that

28 He's strong. _____ you, he's not very fast.
   a) Know   **b)** Listen   **c)** Mind

29 I like meat. _____ said that, I don't eat it often.
   a) Having   **b)** After   **c)** But

30 He's old, but looking at it another _____, he's experienced.
   a) light   **b)** time   **c)** way

RESULT   /30

9) INSPIRATION

VOCABULARY

ADJECTIVES: THE ARTS

1 A Add the missing letters to complete the adjectives in questions 1–12.

1 Which Dutch artist's work was unpopular in his lifetime but is now so w_ _ _ _-r_ _ _ _ _v_ _d that it sells for millions?

2 Whose st_ _k_ _g 19th-century statue is called *The Thinker*?

3 Which unc_ _ _v_ _ _ _ _ _al 20th-century Spanish artist was known for his brilliant paintings and long, curled moustache?

4 Which 2009 film, described by one critic as 'ov_ _ _r_ _ _ _d', broke all box office records?

5 Which off_ _ _ _t actor has played a pirate, a chocolate factory owner and a man who has scissors instead of hands?

6 Which actress won an Oscar playing a boy and then won another one five years later for her poi_ _ _ _nt performance as a doomed boxer?

7 Which English band, formed in 1962, has released over 100 singles and performed a st_ _ _ _ _ng concert, completely free, to 1.5 million people on Copacabana Beach, Rio de Janeiro in 2006?

8 Which iconic Jamaican singer wrote th_ _ _ _ht-pr_ _ _ _k_ng songs about social issues and died at thirty-six?

9 Which U.S. singer, who once wore a dress made from meat, is definitely *not* famous for her su_ _ _ _ _ dress sense?

10 What c_m_ _ _ll_ng 2003 thriller by Dan Brown uses the name of an Italian Renaissance genius in its title?

11 Who wrote the bl_ _ _k Swedish crime trilogy *The Girl with the Dragon Tattoo*, *The Girl who Played with Fire* and *The Girl who Kicked the Hornet's Nest*?

12 Which ch_ _ _ _ _ng doctor in Robert Louis Stevenson's story of 1886 turns into a monstrous murderer at night?

B Match the questions with the answers.

a) Lady Gaga   g) Bob Marley
b) *Avatar*   h) Johnny Depp
c) *The Da Vinci Code*   i) Vincent van Gogh
d) Hilary Swank   j) The Rolling Stones
e) Auguste Rodin   k) Stieg Larsson
f) Salvador Dalí   l) Dr Jekyll

C ▶ **9.1** Listen and check.

GRAMMAR

TENSES FOR UNREAL SITUATIONS

2 Complete the text with the words in the box.

| about | as | did | had | rather | supposing |
| if | time | wanted | was | | |

Living statues

Imagine you ¹_____ to stand stock still all day in 90-degree heat, with pigeons pecking at your feet and small children poking you. And then ²_____ you did it while wearing full-body make-up and a Charlie Chaplin suit. Being a living statue cannot be the easiest job in the world. What's more, the people under the masks are misunderstood souls.

'It's ³_____ people realised this is a form of street theatre,' says Zach Demetri, who plies his trade as a living statue in Los Angeles. 'It dates from centuries ago.'

I ask him, 'What are the biggest annoyances?'

'Well, I'd ⁴_____ kids didn't come up and hit me to see if I'm real. And some people treat me ⁵_____ if I was a dog but, hey, it comes with the territory. I'd sooner they ⁶_____ that than ignored me. And as long as they put some money in the hat, it's fine.'

Raul Castaneda, a half-English, half-Spanish living statue who works on Las Ramblas, Barcelona, says, 'The main problem is your friends and family. They're always saying, 'Isn't it ⁷_____ time you got a proper job?' Well, yeah, I wish I ⁸_____ on Broadway acting with Kevin Spacey and Al Pacino, but it hasn't happened yet and I've got to eat.'

I meet another living statue, Paulina Robards, better known as The White Angel, from Camden, London, and ask, 'What if I ⁹_____ to do your job, what advice would you give me?'

'Find a character you love, study make-up and costume, choose a pose you can hold easily, and learn to control your breathing. It's not as ¹⁰_____ you have to do much while you're in character, but you need to be in a calm mental state. Almost Zen.'

3 Write sentences that have a similar meaning to sentences 1–6. Use the phrases in the box and your own words.

| about time I | as if he | imagine | rather |
| supposing we | wish I | | |

1 Going to the Manet exhibition would be better for me.

_____

2 I love that painting, but I'm not rich enough to buy it.

_____

3 You would think he was a famous artist, the way he acts.

_____

4 If we borrowed his car, would he mind?

_____

5 This computer's ancient. I should buy myself a new one.

_____

6 Picture this: you have twenty-four hours to live. What would you do?

_____

LISTENING

4 A Look at the photos. Why do you think people find them inspiring?

Muhammad Ali and Sonny Liston

Bobby Moore and Pelé

B ▶ 9.2 Listen to two discussions, one about each photo. As you listen, complete the notes.

Photo A

People: *Muhammad Ali and Sonny Liston, U.S. boxers*

Event: *World title fight (for Heavyweight Championship of the World)*

Year: _____

Winner: _____

Background to the story:

In their first fight, _____

_____

What happened just before the picture was taken:

_____

_____

Photo B

People: *Bobby Moore and Pelé, English and Brazilian footballers*

Event: _____

Year: _____

Winner: _____

Background to the story:

The photographer, John Varley, almost _____

_____

What happened just before the picture was taken:

_____

_____

C Listen again and check.

VOCABULARY PLUS
THREE-PART MULTI-WORD VERBS

5 Complete the second sentence so that it has a similar meaning to the first. Use the correct tense of the verb given.

1 We'll catch you and then we'll punish you!
GET
You won't _____ this!

2 Few people fight back against her. She has all the power.
STAND
Few people _____ her.

3 We weren't able to think of any good ideas.
COME
We failed to _____ any good ideas.

4 The blame lies with the government.
PUT
This has to be _____ government incompetence.

5 I'd rather support her idea than risk another argument.
GO
I'd rather _____ her idea than risk another argument.

6 It'll be great to hear all Jaya's news.
CATCH
I'm looking forward to _____ Jaya.

7 I've been busy but I hope to read your work this weekend.
GET
I'll try to _____ reading your work this weekend.

8 If you believe in something, you must say so.
STAND
You must _____ what you believe in.

9 It was years before the CIA realised what he was doing.
CATCH
The CIA didn't _____ what he was doing for years.

10 How on earth do you tolerate all that noise?
PUT
How do you _____ all that noise?

11 She's never really done outdoor sports like tennis or athletics.
GO
She's never _____ outdoor sports like tennis or athletics.

12 Profits are the most important factor.
COME
It all _____ profits.

6 A ▶ 9.3 Listen to the answers. Is the stress on the second or third word in multi-word verbs?

*'You won't get **away** with this.' The stress is on 'away'.*

B ▶ 9.4 Listen and repeat the multi-word verbs.

VOCABULARY
IDEAS

1 Match 1–10 with a)–j) to make sentences about ideas.

1 Why don't we brainstorm
2 We were toying
3 What gave you
4 The idea for the song came
5 We've hit
6 Whose bright idea
7 He's an absolute genius, always
8 I don't know why, but it seemed like
9 It's so hard to come up with original ideas
10 I can't believe we went along with such a

a) the idea of writing about your dog?
b) on a new idea for a product.
c) coming up with novel ideas.
d) a good idea at the time.
e) ridiculous idea.
f) to me when I was out walking the dog.
g) some ideas and see where that takes us?
h) which haven't been thought of before.
i) was it to ask my mother-in-law to stay?
j) with the idea of going to Greece but the flights are too expensive.

GRAMMAR
ADVERBIALS

2 Complete the sentences with the words and phrases in the box.

> simultaneously   almost certainly
> annually   a year   on your own
> probably   readily   to record my ideas

1 I use my phone _____.
Otherwise, I forget them.
2 I get together with my cousins _____ for a family party.
3 If you sleep on the problem, you will _____ wake up with a solution.
4 Once _____, on 1st January, I sit down and plan the next twelve months.
5 Spend some time _____ thinking carefully about the proposal.
6 My twin brothers often say exactly the same thing _____.
7 Yoga helps me relax and it _____ makes me more creative, too.
8 She _____ answered all our questions after her lecture.

3 Complete the second sentence so that it has a similar meaning to the first. Use the word given.

1 In all honesty, I simply can't tell them apart.
HONESTLY
I _____.
2 We have a chance to see Harry's cousins every now and again.
WHILE
Once _____.
3 We offered to help when we saw that the old lady couldn't cope alone.
HERSELF
We _____.
4 It was probably my own fault.
PROBABILITY
In _____.
5 She opened the suspicious package with great care.
CAUTIOUSLY
She _____.
6 Let's postpone the whole thing until everyone feels better.
RECOVERED
Let's _____.

READING

4 A Read the interview with New York artist Rosa Rodriguez opposite. Match the questions below with her answers.

Who inspired you most along your journey, and why?
Can you tell us a little bit about a normal day in your life?
What inspired you to take the path of an artist?
What advice would you give to young artists out there?

B Read the text again. One sentence has been removed from each paragraph. Match sentences A–F with gaps 1–5. There is one extra sentence.

A I can't look at another piece of artwork without taking something from it, something about the use of colour, the shapes, the expression.
B There was such a vibrancy to the place, that I fell in love with it.
C Afternoons are usually taken up with visits to galleries or meetings with organisers and emails.
D Sleep more – people don't usually get enough sleep and that saps their creative energy.
E She also has a mission to inspire others to find their creative talent.
F Sometimes you have to work really hard to get recognition and it takes time.

C Complete the sentences with words from the text.

1 He moved to Tuscany to paint. He's really l_____ the a_____'s d_____. (introduction)
2 We were so excited when we g_____ the ch_____ to meet the band backstage. (question 1)
3 She sat in the doctor's surgery, idly f_____ through the magazines. (question 1)
4 I'll see you here at twelve n_____. (question 3)

ROSA RODRIGUEZ: 'FIND YOUR PASSION'

I came across the blog of New York artist Rosa Rodriguez earlier this year and instantly felt a connection. Rosa is living the artist's dream of making a living from her art. ¹_____ I asked her if I could do an interview and was delighted when she said 'yes'. So, here are my questions and her answers.

Q1 _____

Well, when I was fifteen years old, I got the chance to come to New York for an acting competition. Every evening after the competition, I would wander around the city trying to find somewhere to eat. ²_____ It was so loud and scary and dirty and unpredictable, and I was just a young girl from Illinois, walking the streets of New York. I remember thinking to myself 'One day I'm going to live here.'

Back at school, flipping through art magazines during art classes, I noticed they were full of New York artists. So, I made the connection, 'Art = New York', and that was the beginning.

Q2 _____

There are too many people to mention really. I'm inspired every day by the people I meet, the people I see on street corners, the people cleaning the trash. For me, inspiration is everywhere. You just have to be open to it. I guess, professionally, I've been inspired by many other artists.
³_____ And the people who enjoy the work that I do – they are a huge inspiration to me. If someone appreciates what you do, it gives you a good reason to carry on.

Q3 _____

I get up early, around five. I love the peace at that time of day and it's when I'm at my most productive. I make tea and sit in my studio with the windows open. You can hear the birds and the sounds of a few early starters beginning their day. This is a good time for me to paint or work on ideas. I'm fresh and energised, excited about the day. I work most of the morning, only stopping for more tea. By noon, I'm hungry so I have lunch with my husband. ⁴_____ That's the office work. By the evening, I'm usually tired so we'll stay in, eat good food and relax.

Q4 _____

Find your passion and follow it. If you do something with passion, then you will succeed at it sooner or later. So, don't give up. ⁵_____ Remember, if you want to make money out of your art, then you have to look at it as a business, too. Creating art, you can do what you want but to sell it, you might need to take advice from others.

WRITING

A REVIEW; LEARN TO USE A RANGE OF VOCABULARY

5 A Complete the review with sentences a)–d).

A breath of blue at the Miró retrospective

The Joan Miró exhibition at the Tate Modern in London is the first major retrospective here for nearly fifty years. ¹_____

Working in a rich variety of styles, Miró was both a painter and a sculptor and the exhibition offers the opportunity to view more than 150 paintings, drawings, sculptures and prints taken from over six decades of his life. ²_____

As we travel through each decade, we become witness to the struggle that Miró experienced during dictatorship rule, which he communicates so powerfully in his paintings. ³_____

The exhibition is spectacular, informative and quite simply breath-taking. Prepare to be shocked, appalled, moved and then comforted. As Miró once said himself, 'My nature is actually pessimistic. When I work, I want to escape this pessimism.' ⁴_____

---

a) The works take us on an extraordinary journey, allowing us to appreciate the artist's own intellectual, political and artistic developments.

b) We might have thought that we already knew Miró the painter, but moving through the galleries, we realise that what we knew merely touches the surface.

c) He does, and he takes us with him, beautifully.

d) Renowned as one of the greatest Surrealist painters, Miró fills his paintings with bold figurative shapes and exuberant colour.

B Write a review for an exhibition or show (200–250 words). Use the review above as a model and your own words.

FUNCTION

RANTING/RAVING

1 A Beth and Mike are completing a questionnaire. Correct the mistakes in the underlined phrases and sentences.

Beth: OK, Mike. Here's the first question. What's your favourite film?

Mike: *Groundhog Day* is one of my favourites. ¹It's all-time classic.

Beth: What about your last holiday? Where did you go?

Mike: I went to Turkey with my girlfriend. ²It was an idyllic.

Beth: What's the best concert you've ever been to?

Mike: I went to see Metallica in Moscow. ³That was one the most incredible concerts I've ever been to.

Beth: OK, so what was the last exhibition or gallery you went to?

Mike: I went to a contemporary art exhibition in Barcelona recently. ⁴It was the total waste of money. I paid twenty euros for the ticket but there were hardly any paintings to see. ⁵If there's one thing I don't stand, it's paying lots of money for a ticket to something and then finding out it wasn't worth it.

Beth: Hmm … contemporary art's not my style anyway. ⁶It's not my cup of juice at all. What about food? Can you tell me about one of the worst meals you've ever eaten?

Mike: That was something I cooked last week. I was experimenting but it went wrong. My girlfriend was very polite, but ⁷it was awful absolutely.

Beth: Oh dear. And lastly, what's something that really annoys you?

Mike: Annoys me? ⁸It stands me up the wall when people chew gum. I hate it.

B ▶ 9.5 Listen and check.

2 Put the words in order to complete the responses.

1 A: Did you enjoy the film?
   B: of / was / time / it / waste / a / total
   No, _____.

2 A: Don't you just love Charlie Chaplin?
   B: an / classic / all- / he's / time
   Yes, _____.

3 A: What do you think of this one?
   B: at / my / of / cup / it's / all / not / tea
   Oh no, _____.

4 A: Do you like their new album?
   B: absolutely / I /awful / it's / think
   No, _____!

5 A: Did you enjoy Sardinia?
   B: think / the / of / ever / places / it's / I've / incredible / been / I /one / most
   Yes, _____.

6 A: Unfortunately, we got lost on the way there and arrived nearly an hour late.
   B: getting / worse / there's / lost / than / nothing
   Oh dear, _____.

VOCABULARY

EXPRESS YOURSELF

3 Complete the sentences with the words in the box.

crave fly mind rant rave speak

1 Do you try to hide your feelings or do you let them _____?

2 This blog is a great place to _____ about things that frustrate you.

3 I've had enough of him coming home late. I'm going to give him a piece of my _____ when he gets home.

4 I want to travel the world, learn a new language, a new culture. I _____ a fresh perspective.

5 Community leaders _____ their mind about projects which affect their communities.

6 She did nothing but _____ about the new restaurant and how exquisite the food was.

LEARN TO

USE COMMENT ADVERBIALS

4 A Add the missing letters to complete the words.

1 It wasn't exactly difficult. We b__s__c__lly played the same tunes every night.

2 She h__n__stl__ believed that she could make life better for them by being at home.

3 I'd c__mpl__t__l__ underestimated his ability.

4 We s__mpl__ cannot just sit here and do nothing!

5 S__rpr__s__ngl__, they didn't wake anyone up when they came back in the middle of the night.

6 We're __ncr__d__bl__ honoured to be able to introduce you to Professor Kubermann.

B Choose one of the prompts and make a suitable adverbial to complete the sentences.

1 complete/surprise
   We _____ understand. It's really not your fault.

2 incredible/simple
   I _____ couldn't have managed without your help.

3 doubt/complete
   He won the competition. He is _____ talented.

4 incredible/honest
   We were _____ pleased with the results, which were even better than expected.

5 basic/incredible
   He _____ didn't have a clue as to what he was supposed to be doing.

6 surprise/total
   I _____ agree with you. There is no doubt in my mind.

7 honest/surprise
   _____, they didn't even ask for any more money, as we'd expected them to.

VOCABULARY

COLLOCATIONS

1 A Choose the correct alternative.

1 He's a truck driver so he spends his entire working life *at the job/ on the road*.

2 *Travelling off/Walking over* the beaten track can be a great experience.

3 Ten people *set off/set up* on the trek but only five completed it.

4 When we got back to the city we *headed straight/did a trial run* for the best hotel.

5 She spent *a couple of days/ a learning experience* touring the ancient sights.

6 If you want to spend six months travelling, you'll have *to quit your job/ immediate consequences*.

7 Before climbing Mount Everest we went on several *beaten tracks/ trial runs* to test our equipment and fitness.

8 Working in China for a year was a *trial run/learning experience*.

B Complete the sentences with the words in the box.

| epic   experience   headed   quit |
| road   set   track   trial |

1 The mountain guides insisted the group _____ off for the summit as soon as it was light.

2 I'm going to do several _____ runs to make sure I can put up my tent quickly in any weather!

3 The government doesn't recommend travelling too far off the beaten _____ without an experienced local guide.

4 Most people in our group _____ straight for the pool but we went to the market instead.

5 Travelling through India really was a great learning _____ which taught me a lot about myself.

6 As soon as they've saved enough money they'll _____ their jobs and buy round-the-world plane tickets.

7 After six months on the _____ together we knew each other very well!

8 Driving from San Francisco to New York is quite an _____ journey.

LISTENING

2 A ▶ 10.1 Listen to the description of three amazing journeys. Make notes in the table as you listen.

name	where from/to?	how?	why?
Greg Parmley			
Peter Moore			
Sarah Outen			

B Listen again and complete the sentences.

1 Greg Parmley planned to visit more music festivals in _____ days than anyone had ever done before.

2 He planned to travel over _____ miles and visit _____ countries.

3 Peter Moore planned to travel from London to _____ without _____.

4 His main motivation for the journey was to 'blow his mind and _____ his life'.

5 Sarah Outen plans to travel around the world using only _____ power.

6 Her trip has an educational purpose; she wants to inspire young people to learn more about the _____.

3 What can you remember? Answer the questions.

1 What are Greg Parmley's two passions?

2 What did Peter Moore get in trouble for when he was at school?

3 How will the children be able to keep in touch with Sarah?

GRAMMAR

INVERSION

4 Match 1–6 with a)–f) to make sentences.

1 No sooner had he finished talking about her
2 Never before have I
3 Not only do I love classical music,
4 Not until they had reached the hotel
5 Had he understood the full complexity of the situation,
6 At no point did we even

a) but I sing in a choir.
b) than she walked in through the door.
c) he would never have undertaken to do the job.
d) consider turning back.
e) been so insulted.
f) did he remember to check the booking.

5 Rewrite the sentences so the second sentence has a similar meaning to the first. Start with the given word(s) and use inversion.

1 I had never seen anything quite like it before.
NEVER

_____

_____

2 As soon as they had finished the meal, the waiter brought the bill and asked them to leave.
NO

_____

_____

3 If they had bothered to check the weather forecast before they left, they might have seen that storms were predicted.
HAD

_____

_____

4 It was only when they reached the tiny island that they realised how basic things were.
NOT UNTIL

_____

_____

5 We never even considered inviting our extended family, as they don't get on at all.
AT NO

_____

_____

6 Arriving late was not the only thing he did wrong; he also forgot the ring!
NOT ONLY

_____

_____

VOCABULARY PLUS

SYNONYMS

6 A Match words 1–6 with synonyms a)–f).

1 gripping
2 conceal
3 embark on
4 spacious
5 master
6 journey

a) hide; cover up
b) thrilling; exhilarating
c) get the hang of; grasp
d) trip; expedition
e) undertake; set off on
f) extensive; immense

B Rewrite the sentences using synonyms for the words in bold.

1 Hudleston **embarked on** his voyage to India in 1817.

_____

_____

2 It was an epic **journey** crossing three continents.

_____

_____

3 I've been working at it for weeks but I just can't **master** it.

_____

_____

4 It was definitely the most **thrilling** scene in the whole film.

_____

_____

5 When travelling, it's wise to **hide** your valuables.

_____

_____

6 My hotel room was **spacious** but a little old-fashioned.

_____

_____

VOCABULARY
AMBITION

1 Choose the correct options to complete the text.

How (not) to leave your dream job once it becomes a nightmare

Actor Stephen Fry is renowned [1]_____ brilliant comic performances in numerous TV programmes and films but, in 1995, he was [2]_____ spotlight for a different reason. Having shot [3]_____ fame in the BBC's *A Bit of Fry and Laurie* and now living every actor's dream – a starring role in a West End play – he walked out of the show after just three performances.

He wasn't the first star to have [4]_____ an apprenticeship, won the fame they'd [5]_____ and then found the dream to be a nightmare. Seventy years earlier, a young Ernest Hemingway, having paid [6]_____ as a journalist and short story writer, found himself tied into a contract and unable to change his publisher. So he wrote a book, *Torrents of Spring*, which he knew was so bad that his publisher would reject it.

For those [7]_____ becoming an opera star, here's a cautionary tale: opera singer Roberto Alagna, [8]_____ esteem by the classical music world, was booed at Milan's La Scala while performing the opera *Aida* and walked out of the production. His understudy took over for the rest of the performance wearing street clothes.

Then there are the normal people in normal jobs who end up leaving abnormally. Steven Slater, a flight attendant, suddenly became the [9]_____ attention in 2010 when he left his job by jumping out of the plane on a slide. Fortunately, the plane was on the ground. YouTube and Twitter helped him to become [10]_____ success as his story zoomed around the internet.

And for those who [11]_____ aspirations to become a bus driver, don't follow William Cimillo's 1947 example. While on his daily route in The Bronx, New York, Cimillo clearly hankered [12]_____ the open road. He took a detour of 1,300 miles and ended up in Florida. After being arrested for theft of the bus, he was asked why he'd done it. He replied, 'The New York traffic gets you. It's like driving in a squirrel cage.' Remarkably, he got his job back.

1	**a)**	by	**b)** for	**c)** of
2	**a)**	in	**b)** on the	**c)** in the
3	**a)**	by	**b)** to	**c)** into
4	**a)**	served	**b)** made	**c)** acted
5	**a)**	craved	**b)** caved	**c)** craved at
6	**a)**	the dues	**b)** a due	**c)** his dues
7	**a)**	set on	**b)** settled on	**c)** setting on
8	**a)**	held in high	**b)** high held in	**c)** held on high
9	**a)**	centred	**b)** centre to	**c)** centre of
10	**a)**	overnight	**b)** an overnight	**c)** an over the night
11	**a)**	take	**b)** want	**c)** have
12	**a)**	towards	**b)** after	**c)** for

GRAMMAR
COMPARATIVE STRUCTURES

2 Tick the option that has a similar meaning to the first sentence.

1 I'm nowhere near as strong as Tim.
  a) Tim is infinitely stronger than me.
  b) Tim is a bit stronger than me.

2 The light is barely any better here than in the office.
  a) It's considerably brighter here than in the office.
  b) The light is only slightly better here than in the office.

3 The exam was decidedly easier this year than last year.
  a) It was significantly easier this year than last year.
  b) It was barely any easier this year than last year.

4 That car is nothing like as expensive as yours.
  a) It's every bit as expensive as yours.
  b) It's nowhere near as expensive as yours.

5 The new version of the phone is miles better than the old one.
  a) The new phone is way better than the old one.
  b) The new phone is just better than the old one.

6 It's getting harder and harder to find affordable housing.
  a) It's becoming much more difficult to find affordable housing.
  b) It's marginally more difficult to find affordable housing.

3 A Look at the following statements about life-changing events. Three are grammatically correct. Which ones?

1 I had a baby girl two months ago. Being a mother is every wonderful as I thought it would be.

2 During a stressful time, I sat on the north rim of the Grand Canyon watching the sun go down and realised my troubles were nowhere bad as I'd thought.

3 It's becoming more difficult to find work in my area so finally getting a job made a big difference.

4 Losing my grandfather a year ago was traumatic. I was closer to him than I am to my parents.

5 I dropped out of college. The longer I stayed, I realised it wasn't for me.

6 I found religion in my fifties and as a result my life became a better.

7 I finally had an operation I'd been dreading. It was as bad as I'd feared.

8 I recently lost 30 lbs and now I feel than I've felt in years.

B Add pairs of words from the box to the statements above so that they all become (or remain) grammatically correct.

a lot	bit as	good deal	more and	much better
near as	nothing like	the more		

READING

4 A Read the poem. Whose life story could it be?

Life Story

I first saw him in Texas
Guns flashing by his side
An arrow split his heavy heart
He trembled, then he died.

I saw him next in Africa
Besieged by flies and sweat
He died again in dripping sun
How could the world forget?

Soon after, in a trenchcoat
He spied for the CIA
His bullet-ridden body sagged
But he lived another day.

Still young and tough, he hit the gym
And boxed his way to fame
And breathed his last in a hospital bed
And said, 'It's a loser's game.'

He came back lean and hungry
A gangster with a knife
And cut his way to riches
Till a girl cop took his life.

Then one day we all learned at last
He'd played his final part
The papers saw it coming
And they turned his death to art.

'He graced the finest movies'
'He knew what his looks were for'
'A natural in front of the camera'
But the cameras roll no more.

He'd killed a thousand, robbed a few
Had over fifty wives
And seen six centuries pass by
And lived a thousand lives

And all of these reduced now
To a face in a magazine
And Sunday re-runs of his flicks
A ghost dancing on screen.

B Are the statements true (T) or false (F)?

1 The actor's first role may have been a cowboy.
2 In another film his character died in Africa.
3 In one role he shot a member of the CIA.
4 In another role he trained a famous boxer.
5 He played a gangster who killed a policewoman.
6 He may have been ill for a long time before he died.
7 He was probably either handsome or interesting to look at.
8 No one remembers him as his films are never shown now.

C Find words in the poem to match the definitions.

1 to shake slightly in a way you can't control _____
2 surrounded by unpleasant things you cannot escape _____
3 shot many times and full of bullets _____
4 hung down or bent in the middle _____
5 brought honour to something by attending it _____
6 films (informal) _____

WRITING

A 'FOR AND AGAINST' ESSAY; LEARN TO DESCRIBE PROS AND CONS

5 A Read two statements about an issue. Which do you agree with?

> *The paparazzi should not be allowed to photograph celebrities during private moments. It is an intrusion into their privacy.*

> *Celebrities are public figures who rely on the public's affection and attention. Therefore, they cannot complain when the paparazzi follow them around and photograph them for the public to see.*

B Add one word to complete the sentences.

1 _____ **could be better than** being recognised and adored all over the world?
2 **One of the benefits** of being photographed is that it consolidates your fame, but **one of the** _____ is that you can't go shopping or lie on a beach in peace.
3 **On the one hand**, celebrities need the paparazzi but, **on the** _____ **hand**, they also need some privacy.
4 **Those in** _____ of introducing tougher privacy laws say that intrusion into private lives has gone too far, while **those against** say that photographers have a right to do their jobs.
5 **We need to** _____ **into consideration the fact that** people around the celebrities, such as their children and spouses, are also affected.
6 **On the positive side**, the public gets to see that superstars have problems too but, **on the** _____ **side**, such reporting promotes a kind of unhealthy voyeurism.

C Look at the sentences again. What is the function of the expressions in bold? Do they show contrasting arguments, introduce pros or introduce either pros or cons?

D Write a 'for and against' essay (250 words) for the question below. Use some of the ideas from Exercises 5A and B to help you.
Is it time to protect celebrities from the paparazzi?

FUNCTION
NEGOTIATING

1 Underline the correct alternatives to complete the negotiations.

1 **A:** Get in touch if anything needs [1]*to clarify/ clarifying*.

B: We will. I think everything seems very clear.

A: Good. But do let me know [2]*if you have/if you're having* any queries. We're here to help.

2 **A:** [3]*What/What if* we supported your idea to host a conference?

B: If you help us with that, [4]*we'll give/we give* you a prime space in the exhibition area.

A: Can you promise us exclusive rights to the images?

B: That [5]*must be/would be* difficult for us because of existing deals with other clients.

A: What if you cut them out of this particular event?

B: I'm not sure [6]*I can do/I do* that.

3 **A:** So, we'll provide food and drink at a cost of €110 per head.

B: That sounds [7]*acceptable/accepting* to me.

A: Great. We've [8]*taken/got* a deal.

4 **A:** So, our objectives obviously involve discussing the problems with the new building.

B: Yes, we want to [9]*sort this out/sort out this* as soon as possible.

A: We feel the same. We want to [10]*resolute/resolve* this by the end of the day.

B: OK. So what do you [11]*have in mind/have in your mind*?

A: We want to bring in a new contractor.

B: Can you [12]*go to/go into* more detail?

VOCABULARY
NEGOTIATION

2 Match questions 1–7 with replies a)–g).

1 Is the goal of the negotiation to get what we want without giving anything away?

2 What's the first thing I should do after meeting a new business contact?

3 Why should I learn the native customs and traditions before doing business abroad?

4 Can I tell them this is my final offer even if it isn't?

5 What if they want to sell for one price but I want to buy for a lower price?

6 What if I don't have enough information to make up my mind?

7 Can we accept less than we originally wanted in order to close the deal?

a) Establish common goals between you.

b) You may need to haggle.

c) Yes. Making compromises is a normal part of negotiating.

d) Because it's important to be tactful and culturally sensitive.

e) You can defer the decision until later.

f) No, it's never a good idea to bluff.

g) No, the idea is to make concessions so both parties are happy.

LEARN TO
STALL FOR TIME

3 A Put B's words in the correct order to complete the conversations.

1 **A:** Is this offer something you'd consider?

B: to / like / it / think / I'd / about / .

_____

2 **A:** Will the machines be available next month?

B: that / have / about / to / ask / I'll / .

_____

3 **A:** Are you ready to sign the contract?

B: to / need / it / time / consider / more / I / .

_____

4 **A:** Will we get a discount?

B: now / to / can't / you / an / I / give / that / right / answer / .

_____

5 **A:** How long before you can deliver the materials?

B: to / can / that / back / get / on / you / I / ?

_____

B ▶ 10.2 Listen and check.

GRAMMAR   TENSES FOR UNREAL SITUATIONS

1 Underline the correct alternative.

1 Supposing you *were giving up/gave up/'re giving up* your job, would that make you feel any better?
2 I'd rather you *don't/didn't/wouldn't* smoke inside the house.
3 He treats Carolina as if she *was/could be/would be* his secretary.
4 Imagine you *wouldn't have to go/didn't have to go/hadn't go* to work ever again.
5 I wish they *had/would have/have* at least consulted me first.
6 They're late – what if they *misunderstand/'re misunderstanding/misunderstood* your directions?
7 It's about time they *sort/sorted/are sorting* out my computer – the IT department's had it for days!
8 What if *you hadn't/you didn't/had you* seen them fighting? Anything could have happened!

VOCABULARY   REVIEW 1

2 Choose the correct option to complete the sentences.

1 compelling/stylish
  a) His life makes a _____ story.
  b) She is a _____ woman in her forties.
2 thought-provoking/bleak
  a) We were shocked by the _____ images of injured child soldiers.
  b) The article raised some important points. It was very _____.
3 charming/poignant
  a) It was a _____ reminder of the perils of war.
  b) It's a _____ sculpture by Donatello.
4 off-beat/subtle
  a) The pictures are similar. There are only _____ differences between them.
  b) The humour was a little _____, but it was a wonderful film.
5 the idea/bright idea
  a) It was then that we hit on _____ of getting a taxi.
  b) Whose _____ was it to get to the airport four hours before the flight leaves?
6 seemed like a good idea/gave me the idea for
  a) I don't know why we did it, but it _____ at the time.
  b) Seeing her designs _____ the project I'm working on.
7 novel/ridiculous
  a) How original! It's a really _____ idea.
  b) That's the most _____ idea I've ever heard. It'll never work.
8 mind/rave
  a) The show has had _____ reviews.
  b) Don't be afraid to speak your _____. I want to know what you really think.
9 crave/fly
  a) I'm hoping this new course will help to give me the new perspective I _____.
  b) Don't hold back, just let your feelings _____.

GRAMMAR   ADVERBIALS

3 Complete the story with the adverbials in the box.

> for his idea   on his own   quite possibly
> in five months   readily   not surprisingly

Self-published author hits one million Kindle sales

When John Locke had the inspiration for his novel, he wasn't sure if a publisher would back him so he decided to publish the book [1]_____ using Kindle's direct publishing. He was soon rewarded [2]_____; people [3]_____ bought his novel at only $0.99 each, making it a best-seller. Before he knew it, he had made the best-seller list at Amazon, having sold more than one million e-books for Kindle. [4]_____, this prompted the publishing of his next title 'How I sold a million e-books [5]_____' – a how-to guide for other would-be writers who may have similar ideas. It's a title which could [6]_____ guarantee the writer yet another million sales.

VOCABULARY PLUS   THREE-PART MULTI-WORD VERBS

4 Complete the sentences with a suitable particle.

1 I don't generally go _____ for that kind of thing.
2 We need to come _____ with a few good ideas.
3 I guess we just have to put it _____ to experience.
4 That's outrageous! I can't believe he thought he would get away _____ the crime.
5 I always try to stand _____ for the underdog.
6 I have a long list of things that I never seem to get _____ to doing.
7 The other boy was nearly twice his height but Jim stood _____ to him all the same.
8 It all comes _____ to finances in the end.
9 I'm sorry I can't make it but I need to catch _____ with some work.
10 I'm not going to put _____ with it any longer. I've had enough.

VOCABULARY REVIEW 2

5 Complete the text with the words in the box.

after	craved	deferred	dues	esteem	epic	haggling	job
make	off	overnight	renowned	served	set	shot	spotlight

Max Waller always wanted to travel. As a child, he hankered ¹_____ the wild plains, the great deserts and ancient civilisations. Aged ten, he developed a fascination for maps. Where other children had posters of football stars or singers, maps covered his bedroom walls and he would spend hours and hours studying them. At school, Max became ²_____ for his knowledge of countries and capitals. His geography teacher, Mrs Carson, impressed by Max's expertise, gave him a leather-bound atlas and held him in such high ³_____ that she invited the fourteen-year-old to teach a class of younger children. Locally, he ⁴_____ to fame when he won a geography competition. Enjoying his moment in the ⁵_____, he told a reporter that he was ⁶_____ on becoming either a travel writer or an anthropologist.

But somehow it never happened. After graduating, Max had to support the family after his father became ill so he ⁷_____ his plans to travel. He ⁸_____ an apprenticeship in a paper mill and took a job on the factory floor. He ⁹_____ the open road but with four younger siblings to support, he knew he needed to stay. Working life was hard but through hard work and positive thinking, he prospered. Ten years passed, then twenty, then thirty and, having paid his ¹⁰_____ and worked his way up through the company, he became Managing Director. His parents were long gone and his siblings were grown up but he still had his own family to support.

Finally, at the age of seventy, Max was able to quit his ¹¹_____ and embark on the ¹²_____ journey he had been dreaming of all those years. Travelling to thirty countries in one year, he wrote a blog which became an ¹³_____ success. It included accounts of being held up at gunpoint, going on camel rides at dawn, sitting in canvas tents drinking tea with bandits and ¹⁴_____ with street vendors. On his return, he said, 'I had to ¹⁵_____ compromises in life. It was my duty. But I held onto my dream to travel ¹⁶_____ the beaten track and I made it come true. Mrs Carson would have been proud of me.'

FUNCTION RANTING/RAVING

6 Match 1–6 with a)–f) to make sentences.

1 I couldn't believe my
2 It's an all-time
3 People texting in the cinema drives
4 If there's one thing I can't stand
5 I'm afraid it's just not
6 It was one of the most incredible

a) classic of a film.
b) me up the wall.
c) it's sitting through a really boring film.
d) my cup of tea at all.
e) sights I've ever seen.
f) luck when the tickets arrived.

GRAMMAR INVERSION

7 Tick the correct sentence.

1 a) No longer they would accept his excuses.
  b) No longer would they accept his excuses.
2 a) Not until we'd got far away did we look back.
  b) Not until we'd got far away we did look back.
3 a) Had I been more alert, would I have stopped the thief.
  b) Had I been more alert, I would have stopped the thief.
4 a) Never before had they seen such a beautiful lake.
  b) Never before they had seen such a beautiful lake.
5 a) Had I known about the problem, would I have come earlier.
  b) Had I known about the problem, I would have come earlier.
6 a) No sooner had I eaten than I was back on the road.
  b) No sooner I had eaten than I was back on the road.

VOCABULARY PLUS   SYNONYMS

8 A Complete B's responses. Use six of the words or phrases in the box and any other words necessary.

> complete   cover up   dull   excite   extensive
> grasp   journey   overemphasise   thrilling
> tracker   train   undertake

1 **A:** I found the film absolutely gripping.
   B: Yes, I thought it was quite _____.
2 **A:** Why are you wearing long sleeves on such a hot day?
   B: I've got an interview and I want to _____ my tattoos.
3 **A:** The book's about an expedition made in the eighteenth century.
   B: Oh, so it's about a _____.
4 **A:** I need to get some travel information about Lesotho.
   B: Ask Dan. He's got an _____ collection of maps and travel guides from all over the world.
5 **A:** We're about to embark on the trip of our lives.
   B: It's quite a journey to _____.
6 **A:** I find it hard to get the hang of the principles behind modern art.
   B: Me too. I've never managed to _____ them.

B Find words or phrases in the completed conversations in Exercise 8A that match the synonyms.

1 to conceal   _____
2 to set off on   _____
3 immense   _____
4 a trip   _____
5 to master   _____
6 exhilarating   _____

GRAMMAR   COMPARATIVE STRUCTURES

9 Write one word in each gap to complete the letter.

Dear Noam,

Thanks for the photo. Sad to say, I look nothing ¹_____ I did in the seventies! I had considerably ²_____ hair in those hippy days and I'm ³_____ lot fatter now, too! But, as you suggested, I'm ⁴_____ bit as determined as I was then and I'm still organising, though I find it a ⁵_____ deal harder than it used to be. We tried to put together a workers' forum last year but barely ⁶_____ workers came. It's just getting more and ⁷_____ difficult to interest people in political issues. The harder you try, ⁸_____ fewer people show up. Maybe it's because the younger generation have so much; they are ⁹_____ near as engaged as we were. To be honest, I'm a ¹⁰_____ fed up with banging my head against a brick wall. But I guess that's what it takes to change society.

Best wishes,

Paulo

FUNCTION   NEGOTIATING

10 Find and correct eight mistakes in the sentences below.

1 We want to sort out as soon as possible.
2 We want to resolve this by the end of the day.
3 What do you have on mind?
4 Can you get into more detail?
5 If you do this for us, we'll give you a better price.
6 If what we supported your idea?
7 That would be difficult for me because of the cost.
8 I'm not sure I can do that.
9 Good. That sounds accepting to me.
10 Great. We've taken a deal.
11 Let me know when you have any queries.
12 Get in touch if anything needs clarified.

CHECK

Circle the correct option to complete the sentences.

1 The artist used _____ range of greys and greens to paint the sea.
a) a well-received   **b)** an overrated   **c)** a subtle

2 It was a very _____ article about society's attitude to warfare.
a) stunning   **b)** thought-provoking   **c)** stylish

3 I really think it's _____ you told your boss the truth.
a) about time   **b)** the about time   **c)** about the time

4 I'd rather _____ until the end, if that's OK.
a) we would wait   **b)** waited   **c)** we waited

5 Imagine if you could read people's minds, _____ be useful?
a) that would have   **b)** wouldn't that have
c) wouldn't that

6 We arranged to have a picnic, which _____ a good idea at the time.
a) seems as it   **b)** seemed like   **c)** seemed being

7 Then we _____ the idea of inviting everyone to our house.
a) hit on   **b)** hit   **c)** hit around

8 The live concert will be broadcast _____ on television and radio.
a) simultaneously   **b)** eventually   **c)** readily

9 The jazz festival is held _____ in July.
a) every years   **b)** all the time   **c)** annually

10 We go on holiday _____ each year.
a) most probably   **b)** at the same time
c) simultaneously

11 You just need to be yourself and _____ your mind.
a) say   **b)** talk   **c)** speak

12 If it happens again, I'm going to give them a _____ of my mind.
a) piece   **b)** slice   **c)** bit

13 It's one of the most _____ buildings on earth.
a) subtle   **b)** spectacular   **c)** poor

14 I can't understand who would buy that. It's just not my _____ of tea.
a) pot   **b)** mug   **c)** cup

15 We went to the Glastonbury festival and it was _____.
a) awesome   **b)** the most incredible
c) not my kind thing

16 I'm going out for a _____ on my new bike before the race next weekend.
a) beaten track   **b)** trial run
c) learning experience

17 The doctor was held in _____ esteem.
a) high   **b)** good   **c)** top

18 We should all learn to _____ compromises.
a) take   **b)** make   **c)** do

19 No _____ had I left the tent than it started raining.
a) longer   **b)** way   **c)** sooner

20 At no point _____ I think I'd get the job until I entered the room.
a) did   **b)** had   **c)** can

21 Had I _____ the instructions, I'd have done better.
a) been   **b)** known   **c)** understood

22 We _____ off on this journey a year ago.
a) took   **b)** went   **c)** set

23 Never _____ an expedition without checking all your equipment first.
a) extract   **b)** get the hang of   **c)** embark on

24 That book is every _____ as good as you said it was.
a) way   **b)** bit   **c)** part

25 The more you practise, the _____ you become.
a) better   **b)** more   **c)** best

26 There were _____ any people at last night's party.
a) seldom   **b)** bare   **c)** barely

27 I'm nowhere _____ as aggressive as I used to be.
a) near   **b)** like   **c)** but

28 Do you have a particular plan in _____?
a) head   **b)** action   **c)** mind

29 This agreement sounds _____ to me.
a) accurate   **b)** accepted   **c)** acceptable

30 _____ in touch if you need any more information.
a) Write   **b)** Get   **c)** Be

RESULT   /30

AUDIO SCRIPTS

UNIT 1 Recording 1

1 My name is Felipe. When I started school in Texas in 1942 my name was promptly changed to Philip in the way that all foreign names were Americanised in those days. So, I was Philip Hernandez until 1966. That same year, I decided to revert to Felipe. It was, I suppose, an act of defiance, a political act, because we Chicanos wanted to be recognised for who we were, for our ancestry and our roots. So while my identity on all my documents remained as Philip Hernandez, I insisted on being called Felipe to my face, and I still do.

2 If I told you my name, you probably wouldn't believe it. My parents were hippies, which probably explains why they called me Starchild Summer Rainflower Davies. Even by hippie standards, I thought that was pretty extreme. As soon as I left home, I changed my name. I am now plain old Summer Davies.

3 My name is the result of a compromise between my parents. My mother wanted to call me David and my dad wanted to call me Donald. Apparently, they argued over it and neither would give way, so eventually they called me David Donald. They soon realised this was too long. Can you imagine trying to get a kid's attention by shouting 'David Donald'? So they started calling me DD. Now everyone calls me DD and no one outside my immediate family actually knows my real name.

4 My name is Niamh. It's an Irish name. The thing about it is, it's spelled N-I-A-M-H, but pronounced *Neeve*, which is incredibly confusing for people. They just have no idea how to pronounce it. They say Nigh Am or Knee Am or Nigh Aim. It's just impossible unless you know. But once you know, it's easy. You just say *knee* and put a 'v' on the end.

5 My name is Bond. James Bond. No, it really is. I would say it's been a mixed blessing. It's always a good conversation starter and people immediately smile when I tell them. But then there are other people who either don't believe me or think I changed my name as some sort of way to attract attention. My parents, Richard and Judith Bond, called me James long before the character became famous, so it really wasn't their fault. At one point I did momentarily think of just using my middle name, Terrence, so I'd be Terrence Bond, but then I thought, 'No, why should I? I'm James Bond'. That's good enough for me.

6 My name is Mary Sharf, S-H-A-R-F, which is a nightmare for spell-check. When I first started using a computer it was always changing my name to Sharp or Share or even Shark. I think the name originates from Germany or somewhere in Eastern Europe, but I'm not sure. It's been lost in the mists of time.

UNIT 1 Recording 2

F = Francesca   A = Anna

F: Hello?

A: Hi Francesca. It's Anna. I'm on my way now.

F: Great. I'll see you here at about sixish then.

A: Yeah, or, um, maybe just after. I need to pick up a couple of things on the way.

F: OK. That's fine. I've got plenty of stuff to be getting on with here.

A: Really? What are you up to?

F: Oh, you know, I've just got to finish some work and sort the kitchen out and stuff like that.

A: All right. Er … Do you want me to bring anything, you know, any … um … kind of food or anything like that?

F: No, you're fine. I've got loads of food. Just bring yourself.

A: Lovely, I'm really …

F: Oh, there's one thing I was going to ask.

A: What's that?

F: Are you OK with spicy food? You know, chilli and stuff?

A: I love chilli. The hotter, the better.

F: Brilliant. I'm looking forward to it.

A: I'll see you later then.

F: Great. See you later.

UNIT 2 Recording 1

1 I wish I'd studied more when I was younger.

2 If only I hadn't met that crazy man!

3 If I'd had more talent, I would've been famous.

4 I wouldn't be here if I'd listened to my parents.

5 If it wasn't for you, I wouldn't've known about that flat.

6 Supposing you'd won the scholarship, would you have gone?

UNIT 2 Recording 2

My grandmother was illiterate until she was twenty-eight. Born in Italy, one of nine children, she'd sailed to Brazil at the age of six with nothing but the rags on her back. Penniless and hungry, she went to work in the houses of the middle class. She cleaned things. She cleaned kitchens, bathrooms, bedrooms, offices, dogs, horses and later even cars, the new playthings of the wealthy. Thus was her childhood spent, making enough money to feed her family.

At eighteen, she married a tailor. At least she didn't have to wear rags anymore but life wasn't much better. She was reduced to being a domestic servant in her own home – cook, cleaner and a prolific producer of babies – five in all. By her late-twenties, she got fed up with never understanding the letters that dropped on the doormat or the stories in the papers or her children's homework, so she taught herself how to read. It took her a year. She'd sit up by candlelight, poring over the pages of children's books, sounding out the letters. Once she learned it, her life changed.

She had an iron will and a tremendous mistrust of the modern world. She hated TV. She was horrified at the idea of aeroplanes, thought they would drop out of the sky. And she believed the moon landing was a hoax, that these men in funny suits were actors in a studio.

As she aged, she turned into the neighbourhood fairy godmother, a kindly fount of wisdom. Everyone went to her for advice, which she dispensed from her throne, an ancient red armchair with holes in its sides. She had a saying for every situation, a proverb. If you started telling family secrets, she'd say, 'don't wash your dirty linen in public!' Or 'keep your mouth shut and your eyes open,' or my favourite: 'a closed mouth catches no flies'. Once, someone started telling her a long, elaborate lie. She stopped them in the middle and said, 'Always tell the truth. It's easier to remember.'

Everybody loved her. She didn't have much in the way of material things but she gave people what she did have: time, affection, attention, words of wisdom, love. And so it was with my grandmother. She died in her sleep aged ninety. Eight hundred people came to the funeral. Not bad for a washerwoman who hadn't learned to read until she was twenty-eight.

UNIT 2 Recording 3

A: Did you hear about the archaeological findings in Ethiopia? An anthropologist claims to have found 'the missing link'.

B: Really? I find that highly unlikely. Anthropologists are always saying they've made these wonderful discoveries and mostly it's nonsense.

A: Anyway, this anthropologist found some bones which were unlike anything ever found before and …

B: I don't know about that. A bone is a bone is a bone.

A: Yes, but these were a different structure. And …

B: I'm not really sure about that. A different structure? What was it: a human with wings or something?

A: No! Where did you get that idea? It was a skeleton that didn't look like either a human or a chimpanzee but it was over four million years old.

B: That's very debatable. Four million years? How do they know?

A: I give up. What's on TV?

UNIT 2 Recording 4

1 I find that highly unlikely.
2 I don't know about that.
3 I'm not really sure about that.
4 Where did you get that idea?
5 That's very debatable.

UNIT 3 Recording 1

Paris is obviously one of the most famous tourist destinations in the world. For me, Paris is quite simply the terraced cafés, the smell of bread, coffee and strong cigarettes. Paris is such a spectacularly beautiful city and it has such style. There is a romance to Paris. It's a wonderful place to dine out in one of its busy restaurants, watch the sunset on the river and just do romantic things. Wander along the cobbled streets in springtime, visit the markets.

I think one of the first things you need to do to get a flavour of the atmosphere of Paris is just to sit at one of the pavement cafés and watch the world go by. You'll be amazed at just how many of the classic clichés about Paris are actually true. You really do see the most stylishly dressed women walking through the parks with their designer handbags and sunglasses, carrying poodles. And old men on their rickety bicycles weaving through the streets with baguettes tucked under their arms.

Other things that are must-dos when in Paris have to be, obviously, the Louvre, the Eiffel Tower and the Pompidou Centre. But for me, the true beauty of Paris is hidden in its back streets, off the beaten track. This is where you can find the true Paris and live it like the Parisians do. Take a picnic and sit in the Luxembourg gardens. Or stroll down one of the old flea markets. Take a velib bike and cycle through the streets like the Parisians love to. One of the most important things to remember is, don't try and do too much. Take your time. You simply can't rush Paris.

UNIT 3 Recording 2

To start with, I'm going to talk briefly about the beginnings of the project. Just to give a bit of background information, we first discussed the idea of a cultural centre two years ago. The aim of the project is to create a space for people to see art, listen to music and watch films together. So the main goal of our proposal is to provide a community resource. The long-term benefits include bringing the community together and promoting the arts.

What we plan to do is work with local companies to involve them in all areas of the project – design, construction, maintenance and services. While cost is a major issue, our solution is to ask local government for grant money. In the first instance, this would mean putting together our budget plan and after that, we would write a grant application.

To sum up, we feel this is a very worthwhile project for our community. Are there any questions or things that need clarifying?

UNIT 4 Recording 1

Wrong man imprisoned – delayed justice is not justice at all.

Prosecutors in the USA have been forced to admit that they imprisoned the wrong man for a murder committed more than twenty years ago. Another man recently pleaded guilty to the crime and has now been imprisoned. Henry Roberts, the man falsely convicted of the murder and sentenced to fifty years in 1992, always asserted his innocence.

In 1992, prosecutors charged Roberts, a 63-year-old retired steelworker, with shooting and killing his 21-year-old nephew. The nephew had been spending the night with Roberts to try to prevent any more burglaries at Roberts's house. Prosecutors claimed that after shooting his nephew, Roberts then shot and critically wounded himself. Prosecutors also claimed that despite serious wounds, Roberts had somehow managed to throw the murder weapon into the creek behind his house.

Police based their case against Roberts on conflicting statements he made in the days immediately following the murder, when he was in hospital under heavy medication, recovering from his own wounds. A nurse said she heard something that sounded like a confession.

After Roberts's conviction, police got an anonymous telephone tip naming the man who has now been imprisoned for breaking into Roberts's house, shooting Roberts and then murdering Roberts's nephew. Police now admit that they did receive this telephone call but, at the time, did nothing about it.

Although the case against Roberts was weak, nobody was prepared to admit a mistake until the guilty man himself admitted to the murder and provided corroborating evidence. Had he not done this, the truth would never have come to light.

Baltimore's current chief prosecutor, State's Attorney Patricia Jessamy, recently commented on the case, 'Sometimes justice is delayed.'

In this case, a delay was equivalent to the death sentence. Henry Roberts died in prison in 1996.

UNIT 4 Recording 2

1 freedom of speech
2 civil liberties
3 capital punishment
4 economic development
5 intellectual property
6 child labour
7 gun control
8 illegal immigration
9 environmental awareness
10 free trade

UNIT 4 Recording 3

M: So what would you do?

W: It depends, but if I ever found myself in this situation, I'd probably just ignore it and go and catch my plane.

M: Really?

W: Well, it depends how desperate I am to get home. Because if you stop the person, then the police are going to be involved and then you've got a long process of asking questions and whatnot. So, yeah, given the choice, I'd just ignore it. What about you?

M: Well, no way would I ignore it. I don't think I could just watch a crime taking place and not do anything, even if it's just shoplifting. No, without a shadow of a doubt I'd tell someone, maybe someone working in the Duty Free shop.

W: But then you're going to miss your plane because of a criminal who's maybe taken something very small.

M: It doesn't matter how small it is. It's the principle.

W: Right.

M: My preference would be just to alert someone to what's going on and then just get out of there.

W: Oh I see.

M: This would be by far the best option rather than having to deal with the police and everything, so I think I'd just go up to someone working there and say 'excuse me, that man is shoplifting.' And then I'd let them deal with it. I mean, in practical terms, it's not going to cost you much time.

W: Yeah, fair enough. I suppose I'd sooner do that than let the shoplifter get away with it, but, really, I'd hate to miss my plane.

UNIT 4 Recording 4

1 **A:** Smoking should be banned.
  B: I completely agree.
2 **A:** I think you should resign.
  B: That's out of the question.
3 **A:** Why are you leaving?
  B: The fact is, I'm too old for this job.
4 **A:** Will you buy me that laptop?
  B: No chance.
5 **A:** Why aren't you coming?
  B: The thing is, I've had enough of parties.
6 **A:** Can I borrow your motorbike?
  B: Not on your life.
7 **A:** I think mobile phones are a good learning tool.
  B: You're absolutely right.

UNIT 5 Recording 1

1 **A:** Come on! Tell us what happened when you arrived.
  B: Yes, go on. Spill the beans.
2 **A:** Oh dear. That was close. I nearly gave the game away.
  B: Really? What did you say?
3 **A:** I think I might have let it slip that we're planning a party.
  B: Davide! That's supposed to be a secret.
4 **A:** Can I tell you something about the management committee?
  B: Sure. I promise I'll stay schtum if anyone asks me.
5 **A:** They are so secretive.
  B: I know. I'd love to know what goes on behind closed doors.
6 **A:** I can't believe I told him you were planning to leave. I'm sorry.
  B: Yes, you really let the cat out of the bag.

UNIT 5 Recording 2

P = Presenter   E = Ed Winter

P: … it's the best urban myth of all. It's lasted eighty years and there are plenty of smart people out there who still believe it. They say that beneath the streets of New York, the sewers are teeming with a super-race of monstrous alligators. They've never seen the light of day and they live off human waste. Well, Ed Winter is someone who has been doing some research into this and he's here with us today. Ed, what about these alligators? Could it possibly be true?

E: Absolutely not. It's one of those ideas that captured the imagination but has barely a grain of truth to it.

P: Why do you think people bought into it?

E: Many reasons. Alligators living in the sewers is a very vivid image, for a start. Also, it accords with a certain idea of city life. There's this metaphor of the city as an urban jungle, this kind of darkness and danger, and the idea of some kind of subterranean monster fits with that.

P: Where did the idea come from? Is it pure fiction?

E: Strangely enough, no. Back in the 1930s, there was a trend for wealthy New Yorkers to bring back baby alligators from their holidays in Florida as pets. But once the owners got tired of looking after the alligators, they flushed them down the toilet. And this is where the legend was born that alligators were living in the sewers.

P: So there's no evidence at all?

E: Well, there is one true story. A fully-grown alligator was found in a New York sewer back in 1935. A group of teenagers heard it thrashing around under a manhole cover and managed to get a rope around it and pull it out.

P: So alligators or at least one alligator was living in the sewer?

E: Well no, no one actually assumed the creature lived there. It was thought to have escaped from somewhere and ended up there, which is different. But anyway, that was a well-documented case. But the myth really grew wings when a man called Robert Daley wrote a book called *The World Beneath the City* in 1959.

P: And this was about the sewers?

E: It was about New York's public utilities. So Daley interviewed the former superintendent of city sewers, a man called Teddy May. May claimed his workers had seen alligators but he didn't believe them. So May himself went down there to investigate. And what he saw, according to the book, was 'alligators serenely paddling around in his sewers'. He described a whole colony of them living happily under the streets of the world's busiest city. And then he gave his workers permission to go down there with guns and do as much alligator hunting as they wished. That's what he claimed anyway. Now Teddy May, it turns out, was quite a storyteller. He was almost as big a legend as the alligators. Apparently, they used to call him 'The King of the Sewers'. But, anyway, the writer Robert Daley believed every word he said and so once the idea was in print, it took hold in people's imagination.

P: But no one believes it now?

E: Oh, plenty of people still believe it, but scientists aren't among them. Alligators live in warm climates, and scientists are pretty much in agreement that alligators wouldn't survive the cold New York winters. There's also the pollution and lack of light. The only creatures that really thrive under these circumstances are rats and cockroaches. You aren't going to find big reptiles in these environments.

P: Do you think this urban myth will ever disappear?

E: I don't know. People seem to like it. New York's Department of Environmental Protection sells T-shirts with a picture of an alligator. It's also very hard to disprove the myth, unless you comb every inch of the New York sewer, but who's going to do that?

P: Indeed. Thank you very much, Ed Winter.

E: Thank you.

UNIT 5 Recording 3

A: So, what do you think about the issue of downloading music from the internet? How do you feel about it?

B: Well, it's an interesting question to consider. I suppose, if you think about it, everyone should always pay for their music because that's how the musicians earn their money.

A: That's right. Because if you want to listen to music which …

B: Hold on a minute. I wanted to say that the problem is that music companies charge so much for music sometimes. That's why people are tempted to download for free.

C: But don't you think that we *should* be allowed to download for free? It helps the band to become popular and then they can make their money from doing live music gigs and things like that; or from selling T-shirts and other merchandise – coffee mugs and …

A: Yes. But going back to what you were saying about musicians earning money from writing songs: surely they should be paid for that, too? Where do you stand on that?

B: Absolutely. I mean, they can make money in other ways, but the music is their intellectual property and they should be paid for it.

C: Sorry, and another thing. If a band is popular, so people have downloaded lots of their music, then they'll be invited to festivals. There are lots of other ways they can still make money.

B: Yes, but the point I'm trying to make is that they shouldn't have to give their music away for free.

C: It's not something I've thought about before, but …

UNIT 5 Recording 4

A: So, what do you think about the issue of downloading music?

A: How do you feel about it?

B: Well, it's an interesting question to consider.

B: I suppose, if you think about it, …

B: Hold on a minute. I wanted to say that …

C: But don't you think that we *should* be allowed to download for free?

A: Yes. But going back to what you were saying about musicians earning money …

A: Where do you stand on that?

C: Sorry, and another thing.

C: It's not something I've thought about before,

UNIT 6 Recording 1

1 **A:** What will your life be like in 2020?
  B: I'll've become famous.

2 **A:** How will your work have changed by 2020?
  B: It won't've changed much.

3 **A:** What anniversary are you celebrating tomorrow?
  B: We'll've been married for ten years.

4 **A:** What time does the match start?
  B: We'll need to be there at 1.00.

UNIT 6 Recording 2

For a few pesos on a street corner in Mexico City, a trained canary bird will select, at random, a card that reveals your fortune. On the other side of the world, a Nepalese shaman examines the intestines of a sacrificed chicken and sees the future – a technique that began thousands of years ago in ancient Babylon and was continued by the Ancient Greeks and Romans. Julius Caesar himself used a seer to predict his own future. It's said that, one day, the seer read the organs of a sacrificed bull and warned Caesar that his life was in danger. Caesar ignored him and was murdered days later.

Across the world, throughout history, man has always sought to read his future, to answer the elemental questions: what will happen to me and my kin? How long have I got? Where will I find salvation? We've turned to animals and we've examined the heavens for signs, namely in the discipline known as astrology, a science that calculates the position of the stars and planets in conjunction with the birth dates of men and women and through this, forecasts life's big events. We've also turned to images closer to home: our own faces. Dating from ancient China, the technique of face-reading tells us that one's fortune can be seen in one's features. Clues to emotional and physical health are found in the face, as well as personality traits, remnants of past events and signals of events yet to come. In modern China, the science of physiognomy is deeply respected, and physiognomists are trained over many years. Their field is considered an adjunct of medicine.

Another part of the body that can tell our story is the palm of the hand. The idea behind palm reading is that the lines on our hands correspond to different aspects of our lives – family, friendship, longevity and wealth. Some claim they can foretell the events of a person's life by interpreting these lines.

Besides the body, there are also symbolic objects that foretell the future. These include Tarot cards, bamboo sticks and even tea leaves. But the most famous is the crystal ball. In it, a seer watches images that represent future events. Appearing in a thousand B-movies, the ball is associated with the wise gypsy woman in a darkened room. It's a clichéd image now, yet it somehow retains its magical hold over us.

UNIT 6 Recording 3

A = Andy   K = Katrina

A: So, can you tell us where the ideas, the inspiration, comes from?

K: Going to fashion shows and, I mean, out-of-the-way fashion shows, not just the big ones, going to clubs and gigs, seeing what's happening on the street. This is where a lot of the ideas originate from. Kids on skateboards on the Embankment in London, factory workers in Philadelphia, fishermen off the coast of Genoa in Italy. Anyone anywhere can inspire a fashion designer.

A: Right.

K: Just looking around you. Looking at certain celebrities, usually B-listers.

A: And presumably the big names, too?

K: Actually, A-list celebrities don't take risks with what they wear so you're not going to learn much from, say, seeing George Clooney in a suit or Julia Roberts in an A-line skirt.

A: Right. And what about films, magazines?

K: Oh they're great – watching films, magazines, and also looking at other fields is useful. For example, we keep our eye on the synthetics industry. We look at styles in architecture and furniture design because you never know when an angle, a look or a use of fabric might catch your eye. Basically, we keep our eyes peeled for everything!

A: Are there any other sources? Maybe books?

K: Photography books are great sources. Travel – a combination of colours on a sari worn by a washerwoman in a small village in India may find its way onto the catwalks of Milan or Paris. An earring design from rural Cambodia may end up on a film star at a big event and suddenly it's in demand. Inspiration comes from everywhere.

A: And presumably also the past?

K: The one place where all designers look is the past. Fashion moves in circles, and even the gaudiest, most hideous looks always come back in an altered form. The 1980s, for example, is often considered the decade that fashion forgot, but look on any catwalk or in any photo shoot thirty years later and you'll see full length body suits, oversized jackets, high-waisted jeans, all products of that dreadful decade and all given a twenty-first century twist.

UNIT 7 Recording 1

One of the most famous prison escapes must be that of three highly dangerous criminals from California's Alcatraz prison. Frank Lee Morris and two brothers, Clarence and John Anglin, escaped from Alcatraz in 1962. The prisoners, all of whom had been convicted of bank robbery and had previous prison escape charges, managed to escape from the notorious island prison in San Francisco Bay, despite the fact that it was renowned for its high level of security. A fellow inmate, Allan West, helped the three men to devise an ingenious plan, which involved constructing a raft and inflatable life vests to navigate the freezing cold, shark-infested Bay waters and using a series of human dummies to fool the guards during the numerous routine head counts in the prison.

Over the course of several months, the inmates worked together using tools, including spoons, which they stole from the prison work sites to chip away at the ventilation covers in their cells, and also on the prison roof. They used paint kits and soap and concrete powder to create life-like heads, which they decorated with hair collected from the prison barbershop and left in their beds as decoys. It's thought that the preparations took over six months of planning and prefabrication.

On the night of 11th June 1962, conditions were right and Morris and the two Anglin brothers began their escape, leaving their cells via the dug-out ventilation shafts. However, West had spent so much time working on the decoys and other aspects of the plan, that he hadn't managed to free his own vent shaft yet. On the evening of the escape, despite help from the Anglin brothers, West wasn't able to free the escape tunnel in time and the other men were forced to leave him behind. They left the island on a system of rafts and inflatable life vests, which they had made from more than fifty stolen raincoats sewn together. West did later manage to free his own vent and climb to the roof of the prison, but it was too late. The other men had already left and West had no choice but to return to his cell. Morris and the Anglin brothers were never seen again. However, it's not known if the men succeeded in their escape plan or died during their attempt. The story of the escape was dramatised in several books and in the famous film *Escape from Alcatraz*, starring Clint Eastwood.

UNIT 7 Recording 2

A: Have you seen this picture? Look. What do you think?

B: What do you mean, what do I think?

A: Well, would you tell him to stop or would you let him just carry on?

B: I wouldn't tell him to stop, no. Why? Why would I tell him to stop?

A: Well, because, you know, if you, if you let him carry on then you'll, then he's going to cut himself or fall into the river or something, isn't he?

B: Oh come on. Surely you don't think that?

A: Why not? There's water there and he's holding an axe, you know, quite a dangerous-looking axe, actually. I mean, he could fall over and hit his head on a rock or something.

B: Oh that's ridiculous. There's no real danger. You can't honestly think that. Let him fall in the water if he doesn't work it out for himself first. And that way he'll learn, hopefully, from his mistakes so next time, he'll be more careful. If you tell him what to do or what not to do all the time then he'll never learn to think for himself.

A: Hmm. I suppose you've got a point about thinking for yourself. It's just that, as a parent, or a mother, I just think I would just naturally stop him.

B: That's just mollycoddling.

A: No, it isn't. I couldn't stand back and watch him hurt himself. Where's the logic in that? You can't wait for accidents to happen and then think about what you should've done to stop it, prevent it. You have to be pro-active.

B: Well, I'm with you 100 percent on that. But there is no accident here. It just doesn't make sense to me. There is no real danger. The worst thing that's going to happen is that he's going to fall in the stream and get wet, which is hardly a disaster is it?

UNIT 7 Recording 3

1 **A:** … if you let him carry on then you'll, then he's going to cut himself or fall into the river or something, isn't he?

 B: Oh come on. Surely you don't think that?

2 **A:** I mean, he could fall over and hit his head on a rock or something.

 B: Oh that's ridiculous. There's no real danger. You can't honestly think that.

3 **A:** I suppose you've got a point about thinking for yourself. It's just that, as a parent, or a mother, I just think I would just naturally stop him.

4 **A:** I couldn't stand back and watch him hurt himself. Where's the logic in that?

5 **B:** Well, I'm with you 100 percent on that. But there is no accident here. It just doesn't make sense to me. There is no real danger.

UNIT 8 Recording 1

When she was born, the country of Italy did not yet exist and slavery was still legal in the British Empire. She lived on three continents, appeared in the *Guinness Book of World Records* and some say she helped Charles Darwin develop his theory of evolution.

Who was she? Her name was Harriet and she was the world's oldest living tortoise. Born in 1830, Harriet died in 2006 of a heart attack. Something of a celebrity, her death made headlines all over the world. It wasn't always like that. In fact, for the first hundred years of her life, Harriet was thought to be a male and was given the name Harry.

It's believed that in 1835, when Harriet was five years old and no bigger than a dinner plate, she was one of three tortoises taken by Charles Darwin from the Galapagos Islands off Ecuador. Darwin transported them and numerous other animals and plants to Britain on his ship, the HMS *Beagle*, in order to study them. Harriet spent a few years in Britain but was then moved to a friendlier climate – Brisbane, Australia – in the mid-1800s. She was allowed to roam freely in the Botanic Gardens. In the 1980s, when she was over 150, Harriet was moved again, to Australia Zoo, Queensland.

By now she was a giant. Weighing 150 kilograms, Harriet was about the size of a large dinner table and, like most tortoises, she led a relaxing life, eating, sleeping and being stared at by the public. She was, of course, completely unaware of all the developments that took place during her lifetime; cars, aeroplanes, rockets, TV, modern warfare, the Russian Revolution and two World Wars; it all passed her by.

Although Harriet was the world's oldest living creature for many years, there has been at least one tortoise and maybe two, that lived longer. An Indian tortoise is rumoured to have died at the age of 255, although there are no documents to prove this. And Tui Malila, a tortoise from Madagascar, was said to be a gift to Tonga from British explorer Captain James Cook. Born in the 1770s, the tortoise died in 1965 aged 188.

UNIT 8 Recording 2

1 A picture is worth a thousand words.
2 Don't judge a book by its cover.
3 Out of sight, out of mind.
4 Actions speak louder than words.
5 Absence makes the heart grow fonder.
6 Rome wasn't built in a day.
7 Nothing ventured, nothing gained.
8 Practice makes perfect.
9 Home is where the heart is.
10 Better safe than sorry.
11 There's no place like home.
12 Practise what you preach.

UNIT 8 Recording 3

1 A: Having a good time?
   B: Not really.
2 A: See you later.
   B: Yeah … see you there.
3 A: You OK with that?
   B: Yes, I think so.
4 A: Been here before?
   B: No, never.
5 A: Think they'll come back soon?
   B: I guess so.
6 A: Nearly finished?
   B: No, I've still got lots to do.

UNIT 8 Recording 4

1 A: I hate being put on hold when you try to phone a company.
   B: I know what you mean.
   A: They should call you back instead of wasting your time.
   B: Yes, but looking at it another way, you could end up waiting for days.
2 A: Ad breaks during TV programmes are the biggest waste of time.
   B: That's true.
   A: They should have alternative versions that don't have the ads.
   B: Yeah. Mind you, that's how the TV companies make their money.

3 A: In many companies, meetings are a complete waste of time.
   B: Yes and no. It depends who's running them and what they're for.
   A: In my company, we have meetings about having meetings. Everything could be done faster and more efficiently by email.
   B: That's often the case in my company, too. Although having said that, I think it's better to discuss some things face-to-face.
4 A: I hate going through airport security. It's such a waste of time taking off your shoes and everything.
   B: I'm with you there. It's a real drag.
   A: They should just give everyone a full body X-ray.
   B: That's a good idea. That makes perfect sense.

UNIT 9 Recording 1

And the answers to this week's quiz are … hope you're feeling confident! Are you ready? OK, here we go …

Number one is a nice, gentle start to things: Which Dutch artist's work was unpopular in his lifetime but is now so well-received that it sells for millions? I imagine most of you got this right as, of course, the answer is Vincent van Gogh.

Moving straight on to number two: Whose striking nineteenth-century statue is called *The Thinker*? A bit tricky if you haven't seen it, so I hope you got the answer – it's Rodin, Auguste Rodin.

And the last one in this section is: Which unconventional twentieth-century Spanish artist was known for his brilliant paintings and long, curled moustache? Hopefully you have the infamous Salvador Dalí to bring you up to three points.

Now don't worry if you haven't got them all right, let's see if you can pick up some points in our film section. So, the first question to start off with is: Which 2009 film, described by one critic as 'overrated', broke all box office records? I'll give you a clue, the film had a blue tinge. Have you got it? Yup, it's *Avatar*. A most excellent film, I thought!

Right then, question number five: Which offbeat actor has played a pirate, a chocolate factory owner and a man who has scissors instead of hands? All being well, you have Johnny Depp as your answer.

And last but not least, (for this section at any rate): Which actress won an Oscar playing a boy and then won another five years later for her poignant performance as a doomed boxer? Now with a bit of luck, you'll have the lovely Hilary Swank.

How many points do you have now? If you have all of them correct and managed to send your answers in to us in time, you could be up for this week's star prize! Let's move on to the music round.

Question seven: Which English band, formed in 1962, has released over 100 singles and performed a stunning concert, completely free, to 1.5 million people on Copacabana Beach, Rio de Janeiro in 2006? It's The Rolling Stones! Oh, I wish I'd been there – the reviews of the event sound amazing! Fortunately I'm far too young.

OK, question eight: Which iconic Jamaican singer wrote thought-provoking songs about social issues and died at thirty-six? I expect you all got this one right, as it is the one and only Bob Marley.

And finally, before we move on to the quieter round of literature: Which U.S. singer, who once wore a dress made from meat, is definitely *not* famous for her subtle dress sense? If you don't know her, you soon will, as I'll be playing her latest track after the news … It's Lady Gaga!

In the meantime, let's check the answers to our final section on literature starting with question number ten: What compelling 2003 thriller by Dan Brown uses the name of an Italian Renaissance genius in its title? It was actually turned into a film which was quite exciting … do you know it now? Yes, it's *The Da Vinci Code*.

Now for question eleven – who wrote the bleak Swedish crime trilogy *The Girl with the Dragon Tattoo*, *The Girl who Played with Fire* and *The Girl who Kicked the Hornet's Nest*? It's Stieg Larsson. Sadly he died at the age of fifty, before the books were published – what a shame he didn't live to relish his fame.

And now to round up this week's quiz, our last question was: Which charming doctor in Robert Louis Stevenson's story of 1886 turns into a monstrous murderer at night? You should have Dr Jekyll for your answer and hopefully a full twelve points.

Right then, let's see who our winner is …

And the first email we had in with all the correct answers is from Maud Gimmons. Well done Maud! This week's hamper is being sent out to you!

UNIT 9 Recording 2

A Muhammad Ali? The best.

B: The greatest of all time.

C Ali? *Numero uno*, no questions asked.

A: Liston went down and Ali was screaming at him, 'Get up and fight! Get up and fight!'

C: It was unbelievable.

A: May 25th 1965. I remember it like it was yesterday.

B: It's one of those photos that you just never forget.

A: 'Float like a butterfly, sting like a bee. Your hands can't hit what your eyes can't see.'

B: The thing I love about the photo is that it's got everything – the anger, the athleticism, the physical dominance, the pure brutality of boxing. One man's up, the other one's down.

C: What you've gotta remember is, in their first fight, no one gave Ali a chance. Liston was this monster, this ogre, unbeatable. The boxing writers all said beforehand that Ali was gonna get killed in the ring. The *Los Angeles Times* said the only thing Ali can beat Liston at is reading the dictionary. Before the fight, there were rumours that Ali had run away to Mexico because he was so scared.

A: Never in a million years did anyone think Ali was going to win.

C: Only Ali thought he was gonna beat him.

B: And then, of course, Ali *did* beat him.

A: It shocked the world. And then came the re-match.

C: The photo is of their second world title fight in 1965. It's the first round and, suddenly, Liston goes down and no one even sees the punch.

A: Even Ali doesn't see it. He goes up to his trainers in the corner and asks, 'Did I hit him? Did I hit him?' And it becomes known as 'the phantom punch'.

B: The photo is one of the great iconic images of all sport. It shows the century's greatest athlete at his peak. Fantastic.

D: What I love about this photo is the friendship and respect.

E: It's what sport's all about.

F: Two legends of the game swapping shirts on a hot summer's day. Magic!

D: It's just a great photo.

F: Of course, there's a story behind the picture. It was the World Cup in Mexico in 1970 and not many people had colour film in those days.

E: It was all black and white photos until then.

F: Yeah, and the photographer, a guy called John Varley, nearly didn't make it to the game. His car broke down and he had to hitch-hike his way to the stadium. Unbelievable. Brazil won, as usual and, at the final whistle, John Varley's hanging around. He's waiting there with his camera round his neck and he's hoping, just hoping, Pelé and Bobby Moore, the greatest players in their countries' history, both World Cup winners, will meet on the pitch. And they *do* meet on the pitch. And Varley's right there. Right place, right time. Click click. History!

E: It's a beautiful, beautiful picture.

D: It's the sportsmanship that we love about it.

F: The thing I always think of when I see that picture is the respect, the camaraderie and the meeting of two icons. Never will we see anything like it again.

UNIT 9 Recording 3

1   You won't get away with this!

2   Few people stand up to her.

3   We failed to come up with any good ideas.

4   This has to be put down to government incompetence.

5   I'd rather go along with her idea than risk another argument.

6   I'm looking forward to catching up with Jaya.

7   I'll try to get round to reading your work this weekend.

8   You must stand up for what you believe in.

9   The CIA didn't catch on to what he was doing for years.

10   How do you put up with all that noise?

11   She's never gone in for outdoor sports like tennis or athletics.

12   It all comes down to profits.

UNIT 9 Recording 4

1   get away with

2   stand up to

3   come up with

4   put down to

5   go along with

6   catching up with

7   get round to

8   stand up for

9   catch on to

10   put up with

11   gone in for

12   comes down to

UNIT 9 Recording 5

B = Beth   M = Mike

B: OK, Mike. Here's the first question. What's your favourite film?

M: *Groundhog Day* is one of my favourites. It's an all-time classic.

B: What about your last holiday? Where did you go?

M: I went to Turkey with my girlfriend. It was idyllic.

B: What's the best concert you've ever been to?

M: I went to see Metallica in Moscow. That was one of the most incredible concerts I've ever been to.

B: OK, so what was the last exhibition or gallery you went to?

M: I went to a contemporary art exhibition in Barcelona recently. It was a total waste of money. I paid twenty euros for the ticket but there were hardly any paintings to see. If there's one thing I can't stand, it's paying lots of money for a ticket to something and then finding out it wasn't worth it.

B: Hmm … contemporary art's not my style anyway. It's not my cup of tea at all. What about food? Can you tell me about one of the worst meals you've ever eaten?

M: That was something I cooked last week. I was experimenting but it went wrong. My girlfriend was very polite, but it was absolutely awful.

B: Oh dear. And lastly, what's something that really annoys you?

M: Annoys me? It drives me up the wall when people chew gum. I hate it.

UNIT 10 Recording 1

1

Greg Parmley, a thirty-eight-year-old music journalist, has two great passions: music and motorbikes. So, as the summer music festival season approached and he was sitting trying to think of an excuse to get out of the office, he suddenly had an idea. Why not combine the two? He marked all of the festivals he wanted to visit on a map of Europe and joined the dots. Before long, he had formulated a plan. He was going to attempt a world record for the most festivals visited in a thirty-day period. Travelling over 5,500 miles across thirteen countries, his aim was to bike around Europe attending twenty-six festivals and enjoying music by bands as diverse as Death Angel and Trollfest to Sting and Carlos Santana. He decided to write a blog as he travelled and sent in weekly updates and reports to a newspaper as well.

2

Ever since he was a kid getting into trouble at school for drawing moustaches on his classmates' school work, people have been asking Peter Moore 'Why?' and 'What did you do that for?'. People have always struggled to understand why he does things and it's been no different with his latest adventure – travelling from London to Sydney without flying. Inspired by the Hippie Trail of the late 1960s when there was a trend for travelling East in order to find yourself, Peter's main motive for the journey was simply to 'blow his mind and enrich his life'. He was sure to encounter a few problems on the way. For a start, he didn't really have enough money for the journey and, secondly, there were several borders that were likely to be problematic. However, unfazed by these issues, he set off from London Victoria. The book he wrote, *The Wrong Way Home*, describes what happened next.

3

'London2London via the World'. This is what Sarah Outen has chosen to call her latest adventure. The idea? To travel around the world using only human power. Only travelling either on her pedal bike or paddling in her kayak, she aims to travel around the world on an epic journey, crossing two oceans and three continents. By writing for her blog and sending regular phone, video and Twitter updates, Sarah hopes to inspire young people back home in the UK to learn more about the world, science, geography and the environment. People can follow her journey and interact with her along the route. Children at school can send Sarah questions or videos and there are regular educational updates on the blog, too.

UNIT 10 Recording 2

1 A: Is this offer something you'd consider?
  B: I'd like to think about it.
2 A: Will the machines be available next month?
  B: I'll have to ask about that.
3 A: Are you ready to sign the contract?
  B: I need more time to consider it.
4 A: Will we get a discount?
  B: I can't give you an answer to that right now.
5 A: How long before you can deliver the materials?
  B: Can I get back to you on that?

UNIT 1

1.1

1

1 maiden
2 up
3 household
4 after
5 surname
6 middle
7 clear
8 made
The key word is Muhammad.

2A

Recently ~~I'm walking~~ I was walking
through the aisles of a bookshop …
… when I ~~was noticing~~ noticed …
The title is the first thing the reader
~~is seeing~~ sees …
… if she hadn't ~~been changing~~
changed …
That's OK, but ~~I'm preferring~~ I prefer …
~~I think~~ I'm thinking of writing a book …
It's something ~~I've planned~~ I've been
planning …

B

a) Paul McCartney had been working
b) you've been working on your
   masterpiece
c) it's getting harder and harder
d) People in the book business are
   always saying, Publishers are always
   telling
e) I was hoping to find something, I'm
   expecting it to make me millions

3

1 been crying
2 was wondering
3 eaten
4 is getting
5 was hoping
6 owned
7 been doing
8 always move
9 is always telling
10 know
11 are thinking
12 been trying

4A/B

1 As a schoolboy, Felipe was forced to
  change his name to Philip.
2 Her parents were hippies.
3 His mother wanted to call him David,
  but his father wanted to call him
  Donald.
4 Her name is difficult to read and say
  because of the spelling.
5 His name is James Bond.
6 Her surname – Sharf – is always being
  changed by spell-check.

C

1 He reverted to Felipe as 'an act of
  defiance, a political act', because
  Chicanos wanted to be recognised for
  their ancestry and their roots. 'Philip'
  is on his official documents.
2 She thought it was 'pretty extreme'.
  She changed her name to Summer
  Davies when she left home.
3 They compromised by calling him
  David Donald, but realised it was too
  long.
4 N-I-A-M-H. It sounds like *knee*.
5 His name is a good 'conversation
  starter' and people smile when he
  tells them. But some people don't
  believe him or think he changed his
  name as a way to attract attention.
  His parents called him James before
  the name became famous so it wasn't
  their fault.
6 Because when she uses a computer,
  spell-check always wants to change
  it. Her surname is probably from
  Germany or Eastern Europe.

D

1 an act of defiance
2 now plain old
3 of a compromise
4 are absolutely baffled
5 a mixed blessing
6 the mists of time

5B

Irrelevant information: collecting
stamps from different countries
and being proficient in Word, Excel,
PowerPoint
Missing information: no information
about character

1.2

1

1 inquisitive
2 insensitive
3 conscientious
4 solitary
5 obstinate
6 neurotic
7 mature
8 over-ambitious
9 prejudiced
10 perceptive
11 inspirational
12 apathetic

2

1 a   2 b   3 a   4 b   5 c   6 c

3

1 My mobile phone company keeps
  cal**ling** me every day. It's driving me
  crazy.
2 Beatrix is always aski**ng** us to come
  and visit.
3 ✓
4 My aunt would ~~coming~~ come and
  collect us from school and take us to
  her house for the weekend.
5 As **a** rule, I like to try a recipe out on
  my family first, before I invite people
  round to eat it.
6 I have an ~~incline~~ inclination to be
  rather disorganised.
7 I tend **to** agree with everything they
  say. It makes things easier.
8 ✓
9 Nine times **out** of ten, he'll be home
  by 6.30, but occasionally he'll get
  stuck in traffic.
10 ✓
11 My brother used to **be** apathetic
   about his studies but he's much
   more conscientious now.
12 As a teenager, I was always ~~argue~~
   arguing with my parents.

4A

C

B

1 T   2 T   3 T   4 F   5 T   6 T

C

1 caught off guard
2 niceties
3 smithereens
4 aloof
5 surplus
6 taken aback
7 business acumen
8 deficit

5

1 body
2 soul
3 sheep
4 box
5 ways
6 horse
7 kid
8 neck

1.3

1

1 striking
2 evocative
3 revealing
4 captures the beauty
5 provocative
6 iconic

2

1 e   2 f   3 c   4 b   5 d   6 a

3

1 I guess it could be …
2 I'd hazard a guess that …
3 I wonder if …
4 I reckon it …
5 It seems to me that …
6 It gives the impression that …
7 I'm pretty sure it …
8 If I had to make a guess, I'd say …

4A

1 T 2 F 3 F

B

1 6-ish/sixish
2 couple
3 stuff
4 like that
5 know
6 anything
7 thing
8 stuff

C

vague nouns: (3) I've got plenty of stuff to be getting on with here; (7) Oh, there's one thing I was going to ask.
quantifiers: (2) I need to pick up a couple of things …
vague numbers: (1) I'll see you here at about sixish then.
generalisers: (5) Do you want me to bring anything, you know, …
list completers: (4) I've just got to finish some work and sort the kitchen out and stuff like that; (6) any kind of food or anything like that?; (8) Are you OK with spicy food? You know, chilli and stuff?

UNIT 2

2.1

1

1 effect
2 advantage
3 learning
4 trust
5 learning
6 feet

2

1 b 2 c 3 d 4 b 5 a 6 a 7 c
8 d 9 a 10 b 11 c 12 d

3

1 g 2 f 3 a 4 e 5 h 6 b 7 c 8 d

4A

1 wish I'd studied
2 only I hadn't
3 I would've been
4 if I'd listened
5 I wouldn't've known
6 Supposing you'd won

5

2 Although she was at the peak of her career, she decided to take a year off.
3 My tennis has gone downhill as I've got older.
4 I was at a crossroads in my career so I had to make a move.
5 I find a lot of his theories rather hard to swallow.
6 When I joined the company, my boss said, 'You'll go far.'
7 This report says human cloning is only a few years away. Hmm, that's food for thought.
8 He emails me with these ridiculous half-baked ideas on how to improve the business.

6B

1 She is poor.
2 She has a large family.
3 She is from Italy.
4 People like her a lot.
5 She taught herself to read.

C

1 When did she move/go to Brazil?
2 What did her husband do? / What was her husband's job?
3 How many children did she have?
4 How long did it take her to learn to read?
5 What did she think about the moon landing?
6 How many people went to her funeral?

D

1 d 2 e 3 f 4 a 5 c 6 b

2.2

1B

c

2

1 Wild Swans
2 To the Ends of the Earth
3 Zen and the Art of Motorcycle Maintenance
4 To Kill a Mocking Bird
5 Wild Swans
6 To Kill a Mocking Bird
7 To the Ends of the Earth
8 Zen and the Art of Motorcycle Maintenance

3

1 epitomise
2 gripped
3 poverty-ridden
4 poignant
5 premise
6 swamps

4

1 preconceptions
2 stereotype
3 second thoughts
4 an open mind
5 narrow-minded
6 eye-opening
7 perspective
8 convincing

5

1 making
2 changing
3 to be, to do
4 to have stolen
5 to have changed
6 to have to
7 being given
8 having
9 to have reached

6A

1 In fact,
2 As a result,
3 However,
4 Nevertheless,
5 On the other hand,
6 Consequently,
7 However,

B

1 ✓ 2 ✓ 3 ✗ 4 ✓ 5 ✗ 6 ✗ 7 ✓

2.3

1A

a) play devil's advocate
b) sit on the fence
c) speak your mind
d) beat about the bush
e) have a vested interest
f) have an axe to grind

B

1 f 2 d 3 c 4 b 5 e 6 a

C

1 sit on the fence
2 vested interest
3 speak my mind
4 play devil's advocate
5 beat about the bush
6 axe to grind

2

1 If you want ~~for~~ my honest opinion,
2 Look at it ~~on~~ this way:
3 From what ~~that~~ I can gather,
4 ~~By~~ according to the government,
5 Quite ~~clearly~~ frankly,
6 If you ~~will~~ ask me,

3

1 The reality is (that) corruption is a huge problem.
2 According to the results, the experiment was a success.
3 As far as I'm concerned, Kurt is the best candidate.
4 From what I can gather, the company will merge next year.
5 To my knowledge, he disagreed with everything his boss said.
6 If you ask me, his early songs are much better than the later stuff.
7 Quite frankly, I think she's a genius.

4A

1 I find that highly unlikely
2 I don't know about that
3 I'm not really sure about that / I'm really not sure about that
4 Where did you get that idea
5 That's very debatable

REVIEW 1

1

1 comes
2 'm studying
3 changed
4 moved
5 found
6 always teased
7 called
8 makes
9 planned/was planning
10 been thinking
11 liked
12 hoped/were hoping
13 're considering

2

1 **a)** live up to   **b)** make
2 **a)** clear your name
   b) put your name forward
3 **a)** household name **b)** maiden name
4 **a)** inspirational **b)** perceptive
5 **a)** apathetic **b)** conscientious
6 **a)** prejudiced **b)** rebellious
7 **a)** solitary **b)** inquisitive
8 **a)** obstinate **b)** neurotic
9 **a)** revealing **b)** provocative
10 **a)** striking **b)** iconic

3

1 Nine times **out** of ten he'll be right, but that is no guarantee.
2 I was forever ~~have~~ **having** to apologise for his behaviour.
3 Kids are prone ~~for~~ to eat too much junk food.
4 Greg has **a** tendency to be critical, which makes him unpopular with his co-workers.
5 As a ~~ruler~~ **rule**, most students finish their coursework by the end of May.
6 I'll generally ~~to~~ have just a piece of toast for breakfast.
7 She was not inclined **to** get up early on a Sunday morning.
8 When we were younger we would spend ~~for~~ hours just playing in the garden.

4

1 hand
2 black
3 life
4 ways
5 whizzkids
6 busybodies
7 chatterbox
8 neck

5

1 I'd hazard a
2 makes
3 suppose
4 I reckon
5 pretty sure
6 gives

6

1 learning the ropes
2 trust your instincts
3 steep learning curve
4 second thoughts
5 open mind
6 whole new perspective
7 narrow-minded
8 devil's advocate
9 speak his mind
10 beating about the bush

7

1 would never have met
2 wouldn't have had to call
3 wouldn't have just gone
4 would you have done
5 would never have found / never would have found
6 would probably be / would probably have been
7 not going / not having gone
8 'd thought
9 'd realised you'd already done
10 'd never had

8

1 Talking
2 Having spent
3 being
4 to be
5 spending
6 returning
7 to look after
8 to lead
9 winning
10 to hand over
11 (to) visit
12 not being allowed

9

1 You've done really well, kid. You'll go ~~too~~ far.
2 It started off well, but quickly went downhill ~~bottom~~ from there.
3 Thanks for those comments. It's given us some food for ~~the~~ thought.
4 It was very shocking news. I found it hard ~~for~~ to swallow at first.
5 It's no good wasting precious ~~all~~ time worrying about things you can't change.
6 After all this time, I can't believe that they've come up with such a half-baked ~~for~~ idea.
7 I think he's reached ~~for~~ the peak of his career.
8 I found myself at a crossroads ~~decision~~ and wasn't sure what to do.
9 We'll need to put ~~off~~ aside some time to discuss this at the end of the meeting.
10 You just can't afford to spend so much time ~~to~~ watching television.
11 He has an incredible memory – he is forever regurgitating ~~on~~ obscure facts about things he has learnt.
12 We knew we would have to move out of the house, so it felt like we were forever living on borrowed ~~money~~ time.

10A

a) Look at it this way
b) As far as I'm concerned
c) From what I can gather
d) If you want my honest opinion
e) If you ask me
f) The reality is

B

1 e   2 a   3 d   4 f   5 c   6 b

CHECK

1 b   2 c   3 a   4 b   5 c   6 a   7 c
8 b   9 c   10 b   11 b   12 c   13 a
14 b   15 c   16 c   17 a   18 a
19 c   20 a   21 b   22 c   23 a
24 b   25 b   26 a   27 c   28 b
29 a   30 b

UNIT 3

3.1

1

1 picturesque
2 run-down
3 bustling
4 ancient
5 unspoilt
6 magnificent
7 deserted
8 tranquil

2

1 e 2 a 3 d 4 g 5 b 6 c 7 f 8 j
9 n 10 h 11 l 12 i 13 m 14 k

3A

terraced cafés, the smell of bread, busy restaurants, cobbled streets, clichés, designer handbags, poodles, the Eiffel Tower, the Pompidou Centre, flea markets, velib bike(s)

B

1 T 2 F 3 T 4 F 5 F 6 T 7 T 8 T

4A

1 the Stockholm archipelago
2 Midsummer is a good time to visit because it is most beautiful then.
3 radiant green like a fairytale
4 strawberries, herring, new potatoes and sour cream
5 by boat
6 The atmosphere is tranquil and relaxed. He says, 'the pace of life soon slows'. The beautiful scenery and natural landscape (with deer) contribute to the tranquil atmosphere.

B

free and efficient public ferries
tiny huts share a few metres of exposed granite with just the wind and seals
radiant green landscape of a fairytale
fat cows
Wild flowers nod
rogue moose
packed with trolleys
flying off the shelves
Heavily laden cars
luminously clear
scoured by sea breezes
Roe deer skip out of the path of bicycles

3.2

1A

1 b 2 d 3 e 4 f 5 b 6 a 7 c 8 e
9 a 10 b 11 e 12 b 13 d 14 e

B

1 b 2 b 3 b 4 a 5 a 6 b
7 b 8 a

2

1 poky
2 gaudy
3 roomy
4 dreary
5 airy
6 shady
7 chilly
8 gloomy

3

1 a 2 b 3 c 4 b 5 c 6 c 7 a
8 a 9 c 10 a 11 b 12 b

4

1 unprepared
2 understatement
3 overpowering
4 pro/anti-government
5 anti/pro-government
6 mismanaged
7 post-mortem
8 impossible
9 non-profit
10 malfunctioning
11 depopulated
12 pre-Katrina
13 irreversible

3.3

1

Across:
3 abandonment
4 amenities
7 infrastructure
8 tolls
Down:
1 regeneration
2 congestion
5 traffic
6 urban

2A

To start with, I'm going to talk ~~brief~~ **briefly** about …
Just to give a bit of ~~backing~~ **background** information, …
The ~~ambition~~ **aim** of the project …
So the main ~~desire~~ **goal** of our proposal …
The long-term ~~blessings~~ **benefits** include …
What we ~~arrange~~ **plan** to do is …
While cost is a major issue, our ~~resolution~~ **solution** is …
In the first ~~instant~~ **instance**, …
To ~~close~~ **sum** up, …
… things that need ~~clearing~~ **clarifying**?

3

1 How about if we combine our ideas?
2 Let's look at it another way.
3 I'd like to propose a compromise.
4 Is there any way we can reduce the costs?
5 Is there any leeway regarding the schedule?
6 Let's try to come up with a solution.

UNIT 4

4.1

1

1 suspend
2 report
3 innocence
4 raid
5 wrongful
6 crime
7 drug-related
8 convictions

2

1 No, **it's** nothing really. **It's** just that I'm worried about my interview tomorrow.
2 Yes, **it's** about nine forty.
3 Yes, I find **it** really hard to close the safe once I've opened it.
4 **It's** pointless calling him now. **It's** too late.
5 Yes, I'd really appreciate **it** if you could lock up when you go.
6 **It's** no wonder you're tired. You hardly slept last night.
7 No, but I've heard that **it's** a wonderful place for walking holidays.
8 No, I'll leave **it** to you to decide which one is most suitable.

3

1 hard
2 fault
3 help
4 appear
5 amazes
6 wonder
7 pointless
8 appreciate

4

1 It's a long way to the station from here.
2 It's amazing how often we bump into each other.
3 It seems as if we're too late.
4 It was suggested that the inquiry be reopened.
5 I couldn't believe it when he gave me his autograph.
6 I hate it when people let me down.
7 We owe it to him to tell him the truth.
8 It's hard to know if we've done the right thing.
9 I find it easy to get on with people.
10 I'll leave it to you to decide the best way to deal with this.

5

1 unjustly accused
2 a surprising number of people
3 the true story of
4 protested his innocence
5 miscarriage of justice
6 rough justice
7 demanded justice
8 at that time

6A

1 had not committed
2 four years / the rest of his life
3 confessed

B

1 b   2 c   3 c   4 a   5 a   6 c   7 a   8 b

4.2

1

1 d iv   2 g vii   3 a i   4 b viii   5 e ii
6 h v   7 f iii   8 c vi

2

1 had been living
2 won't have finished
3 Have you been waiting
4 had buried
5 not to have noticed
6 have you spoken to
7 will have been working
8 hadn't changed

3A/B

1 <u>free</u>dom of <u>speech</u>
2 <u>ci</u>vil <u>li</u>berties
3 <u>ca</u>pital <u>pu</u>nishment
4 eco<u>no</u>mic de<u>ve</u>lopment
5 intel<u>lec</u>tual <u>pro</u>perty
6 <u>child</u> <u>la</u>bour
7 <u>gun</u> control
8 il<u>le</u>gal immi<u>gra</u>tion
9 environ<u>men</u>tal a<u>ware</u>ness
10 <u>free</u> <u>trade</u>

4A

2 ~~entertainment is provided on the internet~~ *it provides entertainment* and ~~the internet~~ *it allows*
3 ~~find that we are producing~~ *produce* too much waste from packaging and ~~too much of our food is thrown away~~ *throw away too much food.*

5A

He helped to found the Red Cross, whose flag is shown.

B

1 … 'chaotic disorder, despair unspeakable and misery of every kind'. **There was little organised medical care.** The French army had fewer doctors than vets …
2 … an even worse businessman. **Time and again he found himself fleeing his debts.** Even during the early days …
3 … a small town called Heiden. **He withdrew from the world, but all this changed in 1895 when an article was written about The International Committee of the Red Cross.** Six years later, …
4 **From Dunant's early solo efforts, the organisation has grown steadily over the last 150 years.** Today the International Committee of the Red Cross …
5 … buried in Zurich without a ceremony. **His wish was granted.** But fate had the last laugh. …

C

1 F   2 F   3 T   4 F   5 F   6 F   7 T   8 T

D

1 aftermath
2 bloodbath
3 wounded
4 strewn
5 recipient
6 creditors
7 emblem
8 inverse

4.3

1

1 in
2 faced
3 weigh
4 take
5 the
6 mind
7 things/it
8 drawbacks

2

1 Without a shadow ~~but~~ of a doubt, …
2 ✓
3 If it was ~~for~~ up to me, …
4 No ~~right~~ way would I do that.
5 ✓
6 Far ~~the~~ better to be …
7 Given ~~to~~ the choice, …
8 I'd sooner ~~to~~ live here than there.
9 This would be by ~~very~~ far the best option.
10 ✓

3B

1 W
2 Not used
3 W
4 M
5 Not used
6 M
7 M
8 Not used
9 M
10 W

4A

1 b   2 c   3 a   4 b   5 c   6 a   7 c

REVIEW 2

1

2 It was a 15-carat diamond necklace with a gold chain that he'd given her.
3 We moved to the small border town where we'd met for the first time.
4 They bought her a brand new red sports car worth £50,000.
5 He got a large multicoloured tattoo of his daughter on his arm.
6 Jodie bought a tiny grey Siamese cat with a white mark on its face.
7 She married a charming Science teacher from Jordan but based in France.
8 Let's meet in the same Italian restaurant on the corner where we ate mussels.

2

1 infrastructure
2 congestion
3 dreary
4 picturesque
5 unspoilt
6 deserted
7 run-down
8 gloomy
9 airy
10 bustling
11 chilly
12 ancient

3

1 neither of which I've read
2 which case you can come to lunch with me
3 none of whom had heard of Justin Bieber
4 for which we should be grateful
5 at which point I realised he was famous
6 most of whom had been fans in the 60s
7 whose books inspired me to become an anthropologist
8 in which that actor died
9 which time our plane had already left
10 both of whom love dancing, are going to do a tango course

4
2 irreplaceable
3 misbehaves
4 antisocial
5 immoral
6 overpopulated
7 malnourished
8 undercooked
9 decriminalised
10 prehistoric

5
3 the
4 to (to talk to)
5 strong
6 ✓
7 and
8 ✓
9 are
10 ✓
11 very
12 of
13 of
14 ✓
15 for
16 the

6
1 intellectual property
2 freedom of speech
3 previous convictions
4 appeal against
5 capital punishment
6 gun control
7 drugs raid
8 driving offence
9 environmental awareness
10 child labour
11 illegal immigration
12 economic development

7
1 It appears that
2 It's believed that the
3 it will be easier
4 it makes
5 it's pointless
6 It always amazes
7 It's no
8 love it
9 find it impossible
10 make it clear

8A
1 a 2 e 3 c 4 b 5 d

B
b) to the police to get the job done.
c) justice on each other every day of the week.
d) justice, but he was past retirement age.
e) his own hands when he realised he had no choice.

9
1 has been discovered
2 had bought
3 had been planning
4 had belonged
5 to have been
6 had been bringing
7 have been
8 has been working
9 to have come across
10 I'd never imagined
11 I'll have been living
12 I'll have 'earned'

10
1 no
2 doubt
3 given
4 to
5 would
6 myself
7 up (down is also possible)
8 by

CHECK
1 c 2 b 3 c 4 c 5 a 6 c 7 b
8 c 9 c 10 a 11 b 12 a 13 b
14 c 15 c 16 a 17 c 18 c 19 a
20 b 21 b 22 c 23 c 24 b
25 c 26 a 27 c 28 b 29 a 30 c

UNIT 5

5.1

1A
1 beans
2 away
3 slip
4 stay
5 doors
6 cat

2
1 should
2 may
3 had to
4 ought
5 supposed
6 needn't
7 couldn't
8 better not
9 can
10 must

3
1 are compulsory for
2 may be banned if
3 was forced to retire after
4 nobody dared to ask
5 this kind of behaviour is simply not permissible

4A
1 b 2 c 3 a 4 a 5 b 6 a

B
1 poignantly
2 barely
3 endure
4 imploring

5A
1 b 2 a 3 c 4 a 5 a 6 b 7 c
8 a 9 c 10 b

5.2

1
1 c 2 a 3 c 4 b 5 b 6 a 7 c
8 a 9 c 10 a 11 b 12 b

2
1 be done
2 are (thought) to be
3 had (her wisdom teeth) taken
4 is (said that ghosts have) been
5 be paid
6 has been
7 have been given
8 not (to) be taken
9 will be given
10 to have been
11 is being operated
12 made (his son) apologise

3
1 to verify this
2 the conventional wisdom
3 myth needs debunking
4 has been disproved
5 uncover the facts
6 commonly held perception

4A/B
The myth that alligators live in the sewers of New York.

C
1 c 2 b 3 c 4 a 5 c 6 a 7 b

5
2 a) soldiered on
b) carry on
3 a) crack down on
b) slow down
4 a) poring over
b) talk it over
5 a) stand around
b) mess around
6 a) put away these dishes / put these dishes away
b) blown away
7 a) speed up
b) jazz up
8 a) pension me off
b) called off
9 a) brings back
b) think back
10 a) stands out
b) speak out

5.3

1

Across:
3 injunction
4 source
5 whistle-blowing
6 sensitive

Down:
1 published
2 investigative
6 scoop

2

1 What I'm basically saying is that it depends on the final result.
2 The point I'm trying to make is that we can't afford to waste time.
3 The facts suggest that (the) high prices are a consequence of a shortage in demand.
4 Do you think that is always the case?
5 Is there any way we can prove that? / Is there any way to prove that?
6 If you think about it, it simply doesn't make (any) sense.
7 Can we be sure of/about this?
8 Let me put it this way, the company is going out of business.

3A

1 think
2 feel
3 interesting
4 suppose
5 Hold
6 wanted
7 don't
8 going
9 stand
10 another

C

So, what do you think about …?
How do you feel about it?
Well, it's an interesting question to consider.
I suppose, if you think about it, …
Hold on a minute. I wanted to say that …
But don't you think that …?
Yes, but going back to what you were saying about …
Where do you stand on that?
Sorry, and another thing.
It's not something I've thought about before,

UNIT 6

6.1

1

1 c 2 a 3 c 4 a 5 b 6 b 7 a
8 b 9 b 10 a

2

1 b 2 b 3 c 4 c 5 b 6 b

3

1 have become
2 be using
3 to introduce
4 will
5 is
6 is going
7 won't
8 destroyed
9 have developed
10 could be
11 have been
12 aren't going to disappear

4A

1 'll've become
2 won't've changed
3 'll've been married
4 'll need to be

5A

A 5 B 2 C 1 D 3 E 4

B

1 card
2 (ancient) Greeks
3 animals
4 astrology
5 (ancient) China
6 many years
7 lines
8 crystal ball

C

2 seer – e
3 sought – d
4 kin – f
5 traits – a
6 remnants – b

6

1 by
2 in
3 out
4 in
5 at
6 on
7 at
8 in
9 At

6.2

1A

Across:
3 offensive
5 barrier
6 command
8 dead

Down:
1 global
2 official
4 everyday
7 mind

B

1 ~~mind~~ command
2 ~~barrier~~ global
3 ~~an offensive~~ a dead
4 ~~command~~ mind
5 ~~global~~ official
6 ~~mind~~ barrier
7 ~~everyday~~ offensive
8 ~~official~~ everyday

2

1 d 2 b 3 e 4 f 5 a 6 c

3

1 Strange as it may ~~seems~~ **seem**, …
2 Despite ~~have~~ **having** such a huge influence, …
3 Whichever way you ~~looking~~ **look** at it, …
4 In spite **of** the surge in oil prices, …
5 ✓
6 However we ~~going~~ **go** about things, …
7 Even if ~~had we~~ **we had** managed …
8 ✓

4A

1 T 2 F 3 T 4 F 5 T 6 F

5A

1 The number of children outside English-speaking countries who are learning English in primary school has rocketed.
2 There has been a surge in the size of English-speaking communities in both China and India.
3 The influence of the internet on the English language is due to increase dramatically.
4 The amount of information on the internet is soaring as it doubles its content every ten hours.
5 Until now, most internet content has been in text form but over the next ten years Voice-over-Internet Protocol (VoIP) will become dominant.
6 There will be a steady decline in the amount of written text on the internet.

6.3

1

1 d 2 a 3 h 4 e 5 c 6 g 7 b 8 f

2A

Places: *fashion shows* (example), clubs, gigs, the street, (the Embankment, London), Philadelphia, Genoa in Italy, India, Cambodia
People: kids on skateboards, factory workers, fishermen, B-list celebrities, washerwoman
Times: the past, 1980s

B

1 originate/stem
2 attributed
3 this
4 origins
5 result
6 stem/originate
7 lead
8 traced

3

1 about
2 has
3 to
4 to
5 rise
6 back to
7 in
8 have
9 from
10 in

4

1 them
2 ✓
3 about
4 why
5 ✓
6 the (All in the)
7 ✓
8 ✓
9 to
10 ✓
11 the
12 ✓

REVIEW 3

1

1 compelled to resign
2 a banned substance
3 is compulsory
4 dared (to) cover
5 forbidden to leave/from leaving
6 supposed to check out
7 needn't have ordered
8 was forced to land

2

3 were
4 be
5 for
6 ✓
7 are
8 ✓
9 for (for used)
10 ✓
11 ✓
12 been
13 ✓
14 was
15 for
16 ✓
17 been

3

1 game
2 cat
3 beans
4 slip
5 intuitively
6 fallacy
7 verify
8 wisdom
9 myth
10 scoop
11 injunction
12 sources

4

1 up
2 over
3 up
4 back
5 down
6 on
7 back
8 over
9 around
10 on
11 out
12 out
13 down
14 off
15 over

5

1 that
2 case
3 point
4 think
5 evidence
6 put

6

1 will have landed
2 will be doing
3 is
4 are due
5 could
6 'll/will be waiting
7 is going to be
8 'll/will see

7

1 a) may well
  b) bound
2 a) a distant memory
  b) are over
3 a) are likely
  b) the signs are
4 a) language barrier
  b) dead language
5 a) command
  b) mind
6 a) everyday
  b) a global
7 a) the imagination
  b) a chord
8 a) latest thing
  b) passing trend
9 a) risen dramatically
  b) lost its appeal
10 a) taking off
  b) word-of-mouth

8

1 Difficult though it seem **seems** / **may seem**, …
2 … you wouldn't have listen **listened** to me.
3 ✓
4 Strange as if it seems, …
5 Whichever the method you choose, …
6 In spite of know **knowing** her for years, …
7 Despite be **being** held up in traffic, …
8 ✓

9

1 By
2 on
3 in
4 in
5 by
6 in
7 at
8 out
9 At
10 out

10

1 b 2 a 3 e 4 d 5 c

CHECK

1 b 2 c 3 a 4 b 5 c 6 a 7 b
8 a 9 c 10 c 11 b 12 b 13 a
14 c 15 b 16 a 17 b 18 c 19 b
20 a 21 b 22 c 23 a 24 b 25 c
26 b 27 c 28 a 29 a 30 c

UNIT 7

7.1

1

1 innocent
2 searched
3 avail
4 extensively
5 late
6 launched

2

2 What
3 only
4 reason
5 liked
6 thing
7 It
8 place

3

1 d 2 f 3 b 4 a 5 c 6 e

4A/B

Four prison inmates planned an escape from Alcatraz prison using tools to dig tunnels, life-like dummies and a raft made from raincoats. One man was left behind because he hadn't finished digging the tunnel out of his cell in time, so the others left without him.

C

1 b 2 c 3 a 4 a 5 c 6 b

5

1 One problem for the men was that the waters around the island were infested with sharks.
2 What they used to make the raft and inflatable life vests were stolen raincoats.
3 The reason West didn't leave with the other men was because he hadn't finished digging his escape route.
4 What they did to fool the guards was use a system of life-like decoys.
5 It was West who masterminded the whole escape plan.
6 What the guards didn't realise was that the men had already escaped.

6

1 suspicious
2 opportunities
3 renovation
4 reappearance
5 resourceful
6 tendency
7 strengthen
8 prioritise
9 harassment
10 exemplified
11 evasive
12 clarity
13 brighten
14 sympathetic
15 applicants

7.2

1

1 a 2 b 3 a 4 a 5 b 6 b
7 a 8 b

2

1 Having been brought up
2 Tied
3 Believing
4 Surprised
5 Not having been
6 Stopping
7 Amazed
8 not wanting
9 told
10 Driving

3A

1 take some time out from
2 breather
3 mind off
4 unwind
5 switch off
6 your hair down

B

a) 4 b) 5

4A

The purpose of the festival is to raise money for Amnesty International.

B

1 e 2 c 3 d 4 a 5 b

C

Possible answer:
The first line is too formal. It would be better to use an informal expression like *Come to / Come and enjoy this year's Freedom Festival.* Also, the paragraph does not sound enthusiastic enough: the word *nice* in 'a nice event' is weak, as is the word *good* in 'a good cause'. There is an unnecessary passive ('we are sure the event will be enjoyed') where an active would be better ('we know you will enjoy this exciting event').

5B

1 Mike
2 Serge, Elizabeth
3 Elizabeth, Mike
4 Elizabeth
5 Dieter
6 Regina
7 Serge
8 Dieter, Elizabeth

C

1 squint
2 hazy
3 beaten-up
4 criss-crossed
5 vast open spaces
6 vintage
7 winding
8 scenic

7.3

1

1 unsupervised
2 mollycoddle
3 deliberately; unnecessary danger
4 encouraging independence
5 reasonable risks; deal with danger
6 risk-averse culture

2B

a

3A

1 **B:** Oh come ~~off~~ **on**. Surely you **don't** think that?
2 **B:** Oh ~~you're~~ **that's** ridiculous. … You can't ~~honest~~ **honestly** think that.
3 **A:** I suppose you've got **a** point about thinking for yourself. It's **just** that, …
4 **A:** Where's the ~~logical~~ **logic** in that?
5 **B:** I'm with ~~100 percent you~~ **you 100 percent** on that. …

4A

a) I just think you need to take things easy. / I think you just need to take things easy.
b) The point is that we are always late.
c) Surely you don't think that's a good idea?
d) Oh, come on, you must be joking.
e) That's the whole point.

B

1 e 2 b 3 a 4 d 5 e

UNIT 8

8.1

1

Across:
2 years
3 date
5 about
Down:
1 foreseeable
4 intervals
6 outset

2

1 I was supposed to go to the concert but I forgot my ticket.
2 I was about to leave the office when the phone rang.
3 You weren't supposed to tell her the secret!
4 We were meant to pay in advance.
5 I was to have become a doctor but I became a singer instead!
6 You were to be at the checkpoint at exactly 5a.m.

3

1 c 2 c 3 b 4 b 5 a 6 c 7 b
8 b 9 a 10 b 11 c 12 c

4A

The connection between the pictures and the headline is that the tortoise lived through all of the events in the pictures.

C

1 a 2 c 3 b 4 a 5 b 6 c

5

1 picture; words
2 judge; book
3 sight; mind
4 actions; louder
5 absence; heart
6 built; day
7 ventured; gained
8 practice; perfect
9 home; heart
10 safe; sorry
11 place; home
12 practise; preach

6A

1 A <u>picture</u> is worth a <u>thousand</u> words.
2 <u>Don't</u> judge a <u>book</u> by its <u>cover</u>.
3 Out of <u>sight</u>, out of <u>mind</u>.
4 <u>Actions</u> speak <u>louder</u> than <u>words</u>.
5 <u>Absence</u> makes the <u>heart</u> grow <u>fonder</u>.
6 <u>Rome</u> wasn't <u>built</u> in a <u>day</u>.
7 Nothing <u>ventured</u>, nothing <u>gained</u>.
8 <u>Practice</u> makes <u>perfect</u>.
9 <u>Home</u> is where the <u>heart</u> is.
10 Better <u>safe</u> than <u>sorry</u>.
11 There's <u>no</u> <u>place</u> like <u>home</u>.
12 <u>Practise</u> what you <u>preach</u>.

8.2

1C

1 F   2 B   3 E   4 A   5 G   6 D   7 C

D

1 peek
2 precious
3 engrossed
4 stooped
5 damp
6 slither
7 squirm

2A

2 lots
3 so
4 do
5 there
6 not

B

b) I can remember
c) I can remember
d) I
e) remember all the kids from school
f) of the kids from school
g) Do you
h) of
i) Did you
j) happened to him
k) He
l) joking
m) I'm

3A

1 B: Not really ~~so~~.
2 B: Yeah … see you ~~on~~ there.
3 B: Yes, I think **so**.
4 B: No, never ~~do~~.
5 B: I guess ~~it's~~ so.
6 A: Nearly ~~have~~ finished?

4

2 flooding
3 brings
4 holds
5 earliest
6 hazy/vague
7 distinctly
8 vague/hazy

5A

1 d   2 f   3 b   4 e   5 i   6 c   7 g
8 j   9 h   10 a

8.3

1

1 pushed
2 yourself
3 spare
4 pass
5 just
6 hands
7 world

2A

1 B: I know ~~how~~ **what** you mean.
  B: Yes, but looking at **it** another way, …
2 B: That's ~~truly~~ **true**.
  B: Yeah. ~~Minding~~ **Mind** you, …
3 B: ~~No and yes~~ **Yes and no**.
  B: … Although having ~~told~~ **said** that, …
4 B: I'm ~~much~~ with you there.
  B: … That makes ~~the~~ perfect sense.

3

1 But looking at it another way
2 Having said that
3 Mind you
4 On the other hand
5 I never thought of that
6 I know what you mean

4

1 Is **there** anything we've missed?
2 Anything ~~that~~ to add?
3 What ~~of~~ else?
4 Anyone managed to come up **with** any other ideas?
5 Can you tell ~~to~~ us more?

REVIEW 4

1

3 to
4 ✓
5 so
6 ✓
7 ✓
8 what
9 ✓
10 ✓
11 that
12 something
13 ✓
14 but
15 ✓
16 Of
17 ✓
18 that

2

1 set off the alarm
2 launch an investigation into the thefts from the office
3 take a breather
4 my hair down at this party
5 switch off in the evenings
6 mind off all these worries
7 take some time out from training
8 take risks with your money, not mine

3

1 Having eaten
2 Told
3 not realising
4 Not having
5 telling
6 embarrassed
7 having made
8 handing
9 Attempting
10 Alerted

4

2 persuasive
3 glorify
4 Loneliness
5 exhaustion
6 dominant
7 embarrassment
8 reappearance
9 strengthen
10 deeply
11 musician
12 modernise

5

1 Oh come on, you must be joking.
2 You can't honestly think that's true.
3 I couldn't agree more.
4 Oh, that's ridiculous!
5 Where's the logic in that?
6 I suppose you've got a point,
7 How can you say that?
8 It just doesn't make sense to me.
9 I'm with you 100 percent on that.
10 That's absolutely right.
11 I agree with you up to a point.
12 Surely you don't think that's practical?

6

1 hands
2 earliest
3 brings
4 pushed
5 about
6 remember
7 hazy
8 time
9 about

7

1 to
2 was
3 to
4 was
5 to
6 would
7 going
8 to
9 have
10 would

8

2 c i 3 e vi 4 f ii 5 a xii 6 h viii
7 d xi 8 b x 9 i vii 10 g iii
11 l iv 12 k v

9

1 c 2 d 3 a 4 c 5 b 6 d 7 c
8 a 9 d 10 b

10

1 a
2 of
3 said
4 with
5 Mind
6 at
7 other
8 what

CHECK

1 b 2 a 3 c 4 a 5 a 6 c 7 c
8 c 9 a 10 b 11 c 12 b 13 a
14 a 15 c 16 c 17 b 18 c 19 a
20 c 21 b 22 b 23 a 24 c 25 c
26 b 27 b 28 c 29 a 30 c

UNIT 9

9.1

1A

1 well-received
2 striking
3 unconventional
4 overrated
5 offbeat
6 poignant
7 stunning
8 thought-provoking
9 subtle
10 compelling
11 bleak
12 charming

B

1 i 2 e 3 f 4 b 5 h 6 d 7 j 8 g
9 a 10 c 11 k 12 l

2

1 had
2 supposing
3 time
4 rather
5 as
6 did
7 about
8 was
9 wanted
10 if

3

1 I'd rather go to the Manet exhibition.
2 I wish I was/were rich enough to buy that painting.
3 He acts as if he was/were a famous artist.
4 Supposing we borrowed his car, would he mind?
5 This computer's ancient. It's about time I bought myself a new one.
6 Imagine you had 24 hours to live. What would you do?

4B

Photo A
Year: 1965
Winner: Muhammad Ali
Background to the story: *In their first fight,* no one thought Ali would win but he did.
What happened just before the picture was taken: Liston fell down, but no one saw the punch.

Photo B
Event: World Cup in Mexico
Year: 1970
Winner: Brazil
Background to the story: *The photographer, John Varley, almost* missed the game because his car broke down.
What happened just before the picture was taken: The final whistle went and the photographer Varley hung around hoping Moore and Pelé would meet on the pitch.

5

1 get away with
2 stand up to
3 come up with
4 put down to
5 go along with
6 catching up with
7 get round to
8 stand up for
9 catch on to
10 put up with
11 gone in for
12 comes down to

6A

The stress is on the second word in the multi-word verbs.

9.2

1

1 g 2 j 3 a 4 f 5 b 6 i 7 c
8 d 9 h 10 e

2

1 to record my ideas
2 annually
3 almost certainly/probably
4 a year
5 on your own
6 simultaneously
7 probably/almost certainly
8 readily

3

1 honestly can't tell them apart
2 in a while, we have a chance to see Harry's cousins
3 offered to help when we saw that the old lady couldn't cope by herself
4 all probability, it was my own fault
5 cautiously opened the suspicious package
6 postpone the whole thing until everyone has recovered

4A

Q1: What inspired you to take the path of an artist?
Q2: Who inspired you most along your journey, and why?
Q3: Can you tell us a little bit about a normal day in your life?
Q4: What advice would you give to young artists out there?

B

1 E 2 B 3 A 4 C 5 F

C

1 living (the) artist's dream
2 got the chance
3 flipping
4 noon

5A

1 d 2 a 3 b 4 c

9.3

1A

1 It's **an** all-time classic
2 It was ~~an~~ idyllic
3 That was one **of** the …
4 It was ~~the~~ **a** total waste …
5 … I ~~don't~~ **can't** stand
6 … cup of ~~juice~~ **tea** …
7 it was ~~awful absolutely~~ **absolutely awful**
8 It ~~stands~~ drives me …

2

1 it was a total waste of time
2 he's an all-time classic
3 it's not my cup of tea at all
4 I think it's absolutely awful
5 I think it's one of the most incredible places I've ever been
6 there's nothing worse than getting lost

3

1 fly
2 rant
3 mind
4 crave
5 speak
6 rave

4A

1 basically
2 honestly
3 completely
4 simply
5 Surprisingly
6 incredibly

B

1 completely
2 simply
3 undoubtedly
4 incredibly
5 basically
6 totally
7 Surprisingly

UNIT 10

10.1

1A

1 on the road
2 Travelling off
3 set off
4 headed straight
5 a couple of days
6 to quit your job
7 trial runs
8 learning experience

B

1 set
2 trial
3 track
4 headed
5 experience
6 quit
7 road
8 epic

2A

Greg Parmley: around Europe; on his motorbike; he wanted to break the world record for the number of music festivals visited in 30 days
Peter Moore: London to Sydney; without flying (by land); to 'blow his mind and enrich his life'
Sarah Outen: around the world; only on her pedal bike or kayak; to inspire young children to learn more about the world

B

1 thirty
2 5,500; 13
3 Sydney; flying
4 enrich
5 human
6 world

3

1 music and motorbikes
2 drawing moustaches on his classmates' work
3 She will send blog updates, videos and Twitter messages (Tweets).

4

1 b 2 e 3 a 4 f 5 c 6 d

5

1 Never before had I seen anything quite like it.
2 No sooner had they finished the meal than the waiter brought the bill and asked them to leave.
3 Had they bothered to check the weather forecast before they left, they might have seen that storms were predicted.
4 Not until they reached the tiny island did they realise how basic things were.
5 At no point did we even consider inviting our extended family, as they don't get on at all.
6 Not only did he arrive late, but he also forgot the ring!

6A

1 b 2 a 3 e 4 f 5 c 6 d

B

1 Hudleston set off on his voyage to India in 1817.
2 It was an epic trip crossing three continents.
3 I've been working at it for weeks but I just can't get the hang of it.
4 It was definitely the most exhilarating scene in the whole film.
5 When travelling, it's wise to conceal your valuables.
6 My hotel room was immense but a little old-fashioned.

10.2

1

1 b 2 c 3 b 4 a 5 a 6 c 7 a 8 a
9 c 10 b 11 c 12 b

2

1 a 2 b 3 a 4 b 5 a 6 a

3A

3, 4 and 7 are grammatically correct.

B

1 … Being a mother is every **bit as** wonderful as …
2 … my troubles were nowhere **near as** bad as I'd thought.
3 It's becoming **more and** more difficult …
4 … I was **a lot** closer to him …
5 … The longer I stayed, **the more** I realised it wasn't for me.
6 … my life became a **good deal** better.
7 … It was **nothing like** as bad as I'd feared.
8 … I feel **much better** than I've felt in years.

4A

The poem is the life story of an actor.

B

1 T 2 T 3 F 4 F 5 F 6 T 7 T 8 F

C

1 tremble
2 besieged
3 bullet-ridden
4 sagged
5 graced
6 flicks

5B

1 What
2 drawbacks
3 other
4 favour
5 take
6 negative

C

show contrasting arguments: One of the benefits … one of the drawbacks; On the one hand … on the other hand; Those in favour … those against; On the positive side … on the negative side
introduce pros: What could be better than …
introduce pros or cons: We need to take into consideration the fact that …

10.3

1

1 clarifying
2 if you have
3 What if
4 we'll give
5 would be
6 I can do
7 acceptable
8 got
9 sort this out
10 resolve
11 have in mind
12 go into

ANSWER KEY

2

1 g 2 a 3 d 4 f 5 b 6 e 7 c

3A

1 I'd like to think about it.
2 I'll have to ask about that.
3 I need more time to consider it.
4 I can't give you an answer to that right now.
5 Can I get back to you on that?

REVIEW 5

1

1 gave up
2 didn't
3 was
4 didn't have to go
5 had
6 misunderstood
7 sorted
8 you hadn't

2

1 a) compelling   b) stylish
2 a) bleak   b) thought-provoking
3 a) poignant   b) charming
4 a) subtle   b) off-beat
5 a) the idea   b) bright idea
6 a) seemed like a good idea
  b) gave me the idea for
7 a) novel   b) ridiculous
8 a) rave   b) mind
9 a) crave   b) fly

3

1 on his own
2 for his idea
3 readily
4 Not surprisingly
5 in five months
6 quite possibly

4

1 in
2 up
3 down
4 with
5 up
6 around
7 up
8 down
9 up
10 up

5

1 after
2 renowned
3 esteem
4 shot
5 spotlight
6 set
7 deferred
8 served
9 craved
10 dues
11 job
12 epic
13 overnight
14 haggling
15 make
16 off

6

1 f 2 a 3 b 4 c 5 d 6 e

7

1 b 2 a 3 b 4 a 5 b 6 a

8A

1 thrilling
2 cover up
3 journey
4 extensive
5 undertake
6 grasp

B

1 cover up
2 undertake
3 extensive
4 journey
5 grasp
6 thrilling

9

1 like
2 more
3 a
4 every
5 great/good
6 any
7 more
8 the
9 nowhere
10 bit/little

10

1 We want to sort **this/it** out …
2 ✓
3 … have ~~on~~ **in** mind?
4 Can you ~~get~~ **go** into …
5 ✓
6 ~~If what~~ **What if** we …
7 ✓
8 ✓
9 That sounds ~~accepting~~ **acceptable** to me.
10 We've ~~taken~~ **got** a deal.
11 Let me know ~~when~~ **if** you have …
12 … anything needs ~~clarified~~ **clarifying**.

CHECK

1 c 2 b 3 a 4 c 5 c 6 b 7 a
8 a 9 c 10 b 11 c 12 a 13 b
14 c 15 a 16 b 17 a 18 b 19 c
20 a 21 c 22 c 23 c 24 b 25 a
26 c 27 a 28 c 29 c 30 b

Pearson Education Limited
Edinburgh Gate
Harlow
Essex CM20 2JE
England
and Associated Companies throughout the world.

www.pearsonelt.com

First published 2016
Sixth impression 2020
ISBN: 978-1-4479-7666-0

Set in Aptifer sans 10/12 pt
Printed and bound by CPI Group (UK) Ltd, Croydon, CR0 4YY

Illustration acknowledgements
Illustrated by Eric@kja-artists

Photo acknowledgements
The publisher would like to thank the following for their kind permission to
reproduce their photographs:

(Key: b-bottom; c-centre; l-left; r-right; t-top)

123RF.com: ayzek 38tl; **Alamy Images:** Archive Pics 26, Blend Images 63, Judith
Collins 38br, Johner Images 19, National Geographic Image Collection 21,
PF-(wararchive) 33r, paul prescott 66, Trinity Mirror / Mirrorpix 61 (B), World
History Archive 61 (A); **Digital Vision:** 8 (C); **Fotolia.com:** auremar 38tr, Svetlana
Batura 8 (B), dundanim 10, hubb67 22, Jcjg Photography 43t, lornet 18b, Aleš
Nowák 71, philipus 33l, sarininka 18t, StockRocket 41, uckyo 53 (B), vetal1983
39, Vidady 53 (A), Wong Sze Fei 8 (D); **Getty Images:** Peter Dazeley 38bl, i love
images 53 (C), Paul Kane 65b, Soe Than WIN / AFP 16; **Glow Images:** OJO
Images 14; **Imagemore Co., Ltd:** 26 (red cross); **John Foxx Images:** Imagestate
8 (A); **Shutterstock.com:** Albert Barr 38 (background), Tomasz Markowski
43c, Monkey Business Images 43b, Anna Omelchenko 65tl, Paul Vasarhelyi 72;
SuperStock: 35; **The Kobal Collection:** Universal 24b, Warner Bros 24t; **The
Random House Group Ltd:** 65tr

All other images © Pearson Education

Every effort has been made to trace the copyright holders and we apologise
in advance for any unintentional omissions. We would be pleased to insert the
appropriate acknowledgement in any subsequent edition of this publication.